THE ULTIMATE MOTIVATED EMPLOYEE!

7 steps to a more productive workforce.

Gary Brose

> *Special discounts on bulk quantities of this book are available by contacting the Publishing Department at www.smallbizsherpa.com.*

This publication is designed to provide accurate and authoritative information in regard to the subject matter covered. It is sold with the understanding that the publisher is not engaged in rendering legal, accounting, or other professional service. If legal advice or other expert assistance is required, the services of a competent professional person should be sought.

ISBN: 978-1-105-62545-9

Copyright 2012 Gary Brose
All rights reserved.
Printed in the United States of America
First Edition

This publication may not be reproduced, stored in a retrieval system, or transmitted in whole or in part, in any form or by any means, electronic, mechanical, photocopying, recording or otherwise, without the prior written permission of Gary Brose, Creative Consulting Corp or SmallBizSherpa.com.

v7

This book is dedicated to
the one person in this world
who motivates me to be a better man:
my wife, Kathleen.

TABLE OF CONTENTS

Chapter 1: Introduction — 1

Chapter 2: Create the right work environment — 3

Chapter 3: Hire the right people — 35

Chapter 4: Excel at 'Greet and Train' — 55

Chapter 5: Incentivize, bonus and reward — 69

Chapter 6: Delink reviews and raises — 93

Chapter 7: Be the Servant — 108

Chapter 8: Respect and involve — 119

Chapter 9: Conclusion — 131

Acknowledgments

When I first decided to write this book as a more general follow-up to my first book *"Bonus Your Way to Profits!"*, I planned on writing in general terms about the concepts of management and then reinforcing those thoughts with stories of my own. I've had thirty plus years of experience managing small companies with anywhere from 1 to 120 employees. During that time, I've made hundreds of mistakes and, somehow, along the way, discovered a few things that work really well. I have dozens of stories about techniques I have used to motivate workers (and hundreds of stories about methods that failed miserably).

But a funny thing happened on the way to the final drafting table. I started talking with other business owners and managers and realized that their stories were so much more powerful than mine. Hearing about motivational success from their perspective gave greater weight to the concepts.

So, I reached out to others and their response was gratifying and reinforcing. Dozens of stories were submitted and the very best are included. I still added in a few of my own but I love my contributors' passion and unique writing talents. So I want to thank everyone who contributed to the effort. Each one of the contributors is an astute business owner or manager in their own right and they all deserve credit.

I also want to thank my friends: Larry Coffman for his never-ending mentorship and support; and Jeff Angus for his friendship and insightful guidance. Jeff's book, *"Management by Baseball"* has had an obvious impact on me so readers will have to live with my frequent baseball analogies. Friends like Larry and Jeff make me appreciate how great it is to have someone to lean on.

FOREWORD

As a business owner, I have often tried to imagine the absolute best case scenario for running my business. I always come back to the same thing: I want to create a process and structure that the employees carry out with precision, enthusiasm and energy whether I am there or not.

In fact, in my best scenario, I just get in the way when I am at the office and it is best if I simply pop my head in now and then and see what is happening. I want to be able to take a day off occasionally without the fear that the business will crumble if I am not there. I want all my employees to feel a sense of brand ownership and a caring attitude about the well-being of our customers.

In short, I want them to feel the same way that I do about the business. Unrealistic? Perhaps, since most or all of the employees would not be part owners, but the same general sense can be achieved through a motivated work force; And not just typically motivated but "super-charged" with a giant dose of incentives to do the right thing. What I and every other business owner or manager needs is an entire crew of the Ultimate Motivated Employees.

And what we truly need is the blueprint for making that happen ...

CHAPTER ONE

"Motivation is the art of getting people to do what you want them to do because they want to do it."
-Dwight Eisenhower

"In motivating people, you've got to engage their minds and their hearts. It is good business to have an employee feel part of the entire effort …"
-Rupert Murdoch

When Sam Snead was asked how to putt, he said, "Putt for one hundred dollars"
-Bob Schieffer

In business terms, many of us think of motivation as something that management does that incentivizes the employees. That usually means providing pay incentives, bonuses, penalties for errors or failure or maybe just the occasional 'attaboy'. We often confuse "motivating employees" with some singular act that occurs. I have seen managers call employees into their office and proceed to 'motivate them' by ripping their face off for a minor infraction. Far too many actions have been taken in the name of motivation because we don't know what else to call it.

But creating motivation is not a singular act. It is not a pat on the back or a call to action. It is not a public undressing or a private reprimand. And it is not a one-time bonus or reward for meeting a solitary goal.

Creating motivation is an art form. It is a dance that starts slowly and builds momentum. It is a vocation and an obsession that begins the day a future employee applies for work and keeps adding on over time. It is a corporate culture that encourages growth, ingenuity, individualism and the willingness to act independently without fear.

... AND IT IS A MINDSET

Truly creating a motivated workforce is not something that management does occasionally. It is not an afterthought or a series of disconnected singular actions. It is a mindset and a commitment to the principles that generate an atmosphere of motivation. And it begins at the top.

For business owners or managers who are in a position to affect change, there are Seven Key Elements of this mindset and they need to be embraced fully to make them work.

1) CREATE THE RIGHT WORK ENVIRONMENT
2) HIRE THE RIGHT PEOPLE
3) EXCEL AT "GREET AND TRAIN"
4) INCENTIVIZE, BONUS AND REWARD
5) DELINK REVIEWS AND RAISES
6) BE THE SERVANT
7) RESPECT AND INVOLVE

You may be asking yourself *"Where exactly do I begin?"* Well, you start at the focal point. That would be YOU; and your attitude about business; and every action that you take that affects your employees. See, this is one of those times when it really IS all about you! You begin simply by thinking; by reflecting; by learning more about yourself and how the actions you take affect all those around you.

You begin now ...

CHAPTER TWO

CREATE THE RIGHT ATMOSPHERE

"It is wisdom to know others; it is enlightenment to know one's self."

Lao-Tzu

Many of us spend our entire lives learning who we truly are. Some seem to know early in life. Either way, it is a solitary personal journey and, as the saying goes, it begins with a single step.

If you have not taken many steps in that journey, you need to do so now. To be a successful business manager, you must know yourself; know your strong points, your weaknesses, your comfort zone. Take action today. If it helps, make a written list of your pluses and minuses and ask yourself where you could do better. Identify who you are and who you would become.

Leading others in any endeavor requires confidence in your own abilities. It is vital that you know what those are ... and what they aren't. Rely on your strengths and work on your weaknesses. There is no shame in imperfection. Even our greatest leaders were less than perfect human beings. The key is to be honest with yourself and know who you are.

Then, act as you are, be true to yourself, treasure consistency and strive to be who you would become.

"When I am trusting and being myself ... everything in my life reflects this by falling into place easily, often miraculously."

Shakti Gawain

Have you ever met someone who seemed to make everything they did look easy? Did you catch yourself wondering how that could be?

Gawain's insight is an extraordinary statement of a simple philosophy. 'Being yourself' can be a complicated process. Or it can be much easier than you would believe. For those who do not know themselves, it is an impossible task while for those who do it is as natural as breathing.

When a baseball player strokes a single into the outfield, the announcers will frequently say that he 'stayed within himself' or he 'didn't try to do too much'. A weak hitter must know that he cannot swing for the fences and try to hit a homerun. Instead, he focuses on what he does best: taking a nice level swing and punching the ball to right field. And when he is trusting and being himself, he makes it look easy.

As a manager, you too must go with your strengths and stay within yourself. If you are naturally funny, employ humor as your tool. Overly gregarious? Then focus on sales and marketing. If you are good with numbers, put that skill to use. If you are a natural introvert, focus on operations and processes. Go with your strengths, be yourself and life will fall into place more easily.

"A boss creates fear, a leader confidence. A boss fixes blame, a leader corrects mistakes. A boss knows all, a leader asks questions. A boss makes work drudgery, a leader makes it interesting. A boss is interested in himself or herself, a leader is interested in the group."

Russell H. Ewing

In our lifetimes we have all worked for a variety of bosses. Some great, some good, some, well, not so good. When you reflect on those you rated highly, it becomes clear to see that there are common elements among the best bosses and Ewing's quote nails those down for us.

Now you are the boss and others are looking to you for leadership and guidance. What kind of boss are you going to be? Will you be the type that accentuates the positive or will you dwell on fear, failure and negativity?

The goal of any leader is to get the desired results. You'll find those results come easier when everyone is on-board, following your lead and working with you. Create confidence in your employees; focus on finding solutions and improving process; make work a joyful journey, an exciting challenge.

Do you feel like you must be the master of everything? That you must know all the details of the business and show everyone that you are in control? Let go of that. Do as Ewing suggests. Ask questions. Probe more deeply into problems. Show a concern for learning the truth and finding solutions rather than pinning blame and attempting to prove that you are the anointed one who has all the answers.

When you unburden yourself of the duty of knowing all, you liberate yourself and allow work to become a collaborative and wondrous journey taken by you and your employees. Find the truths together. Build your staff's confidence in themselves. Unleash the magic of creating a workplace that thrives on its mutual voyage together.

THE ERROR OF GETTING RIGHT TO THE POINT
As told by Maria Stevens

Jim was a straightforward kind of guy. He valued time greatly and strove to achieve as much as he could in as short a time as possible. In bragging about how many meetings he could get through in one day, he often said to me, *"I don't waste time on small talk. I get right down to business."*

Jim felt like getting right to the point was the correct approach. He was under a lot of pressure for his team to perform after almost 2 years of missing their objectives. Things only got worse for Jim after his mid-year management survey revealed that the people on his team perceived him as impersonal, insensitive, and too hard-driving. Jim was perplexed. He was more focused on the team's results than ever before, but everything seemed to be going in the wrong direction. What's more, Jim sensed that he was losing some credibility within his team.

During our coaching calls, we explored some solutions. Deep down, Jim cared about his team members and truly wanted them to be successful. But the way he conducted himself seemed to demonstrate that he was someone whose only focus was on results not the people who generated them.

It was during our coaching sessions that I challenged Jim to think differently about the way that he relates with his team. I asked Jim to prioritize relationships instead of results. Jim realized that his current way of leading was not working, so he agreed to my requests. It turns out that Jim had been a sales rep himself for several years before taking a leadership role. Yet he never talked with his current team about how he dealt with some of the same challenges that they were now encountering. Jim realized that this was the perfect way to begin bonding and relating to his team members.

To start, Jim decided that he would open each conference call by sharing one of his own stories of struggle or success as a former sales rep. He extended the time of his meetings from thirty to forty-five minutes and worked hard at "relating".

He told me later that he could almost hear the relief in their voices. Jim sensed that sharing the story helped his team members feel like he too, had faced his fair share of customer problems in the past.

Over the course of a few months, Jim observed that as he continued opening up to his team, the team starting talking more openly about their challenges. Over time Jim began to understand the root of many of the problems that his reps were experiencing and he took more deliberate steps to resolve those problems. Trust levels increased and the team became more open. The employees started seeing Jim in a different light and began responding better to his guidance.

In the end, Jim's meetings did last a little bit longer. But the final result was that he went from 45% of his reps making quota to 92%! And, his next management survey showed significant increases in his leadership ratings. Interestingly enough, Jim told me he actually enjoyed getting to know his team members better and that it made his work more enjoyable overall. He invested in his people and in the process learned a very valuable lesson: *for there to be leadership, there must first be a connection.*

Maria Stevens is the founder and owner of Stevens Coaching & Consulting. She is an in-demand business coach, sales trainer and author of *From Manager to Coach: How to Lead a Winning Sales Team.* For more information visit www.Stevenscoaching.com

"Many know how to flatter, few know how to praise."
Wendell Phillips

For many, there is no greater difficulty than knowing how to receive a compliment or, conversely, how to give one. Yet, knowing how to praise is an art and it is one that requires practice, patience and a genuineness of spirit.

Have you ever had a stranger compliment you on your choice of clothing? How did that make you feel? Did you catch yourself replaying that simple comment in your mind many times that day and did you realize that every time you did that, you were smiling?

Imagine having the power to praise someone and cause them to replay it in their minds multiple times. And smile to themselves each time they did it. Well, you don't have to imagine it. You can do it.

As a manager of people, you have a unique power to pay a genuine and sincere compliment to your employees and literally 'make their day'. This is not hard to do but it is done far too infrequently. Some managers feel that too many compliments can create a monster. Or that praising others somehow detracts from their own success. Neither could be further from the truth. The key is to praise generously **when it is deserved**. Do not flatter to gain favor, but praise good work every chance you get.

Try to find something your employees do that you can praise every day. Be sincere and genuine and practice giving praise. Over time, you will learn that each person responds to praise in different ways and you can tailor your comments accordingly. Become a professional at it.

Giving sincere and deserved praise costs so little and returns so much.

ON THE WINGS OF TOUGH LOVE
As told by Heather Sahli

Tough love is a motivational style that many find difficult to execute. I myself found it hard until I had to implement the system in my own office.

Emily was my favorite intern. She had the potential to become a great businesswoman: Driven, intelligent, and full of passion. I had one issue with her - she lacked the level of motivation needed to reach her full potential. I literally sat up all night thinking of ways to motivate her. At 4AM it struck me: TOUGH LOVE. All of the great business leaders have used it. That next day at work I put it into action. Emily brought me a project that was just not up to par. I knew she could do better work. So I point blank told her *"This is not acceptable"*. Her response was simply, *"I followed the directions"*. The conversation went on for nearly an hour. I explained that simply following directions isn't acceptable. There had to be evidence of passion and ample time spent on the project. Passion moves people to action! I spent time going over the project with her page-by-page telling her what wasn't working. She brought the project back to me at the end of the week. The difference was night and day: Clear, concise work full of passion and belief for the cause. I knew she could do it. I gave her praise for her wonderful work. Over the course of her internship her work exceeded my expectations. She is now an executive at a large corporation.

A few things to point out: First, there is a clear line between constructive criticism and humiliation. I had the gracious opportunity to talk to Steve Jobs on several occasions. He was known to make examples of employees in front of everyone. Granted I refuse to go that far, the lesson remains the same. Constructive criticism is the best way to get the most out of your workers. It gives them something to IMPROVE upon. Humiliation on the other hand is just a counter- productive pitfall of a person's confidence and self-worth.

Secondly, keep any criticism related to the job. That also means: DON"T nit-pick. My job wasn't to break Emily down as a worker or person. Rather it was to help her learn and grow into the best businesswoman she could be. The phrases *"This is right but..."* and *"Let's try it this way"* are just a couple I've found to be very effective.

Lastly, tough love isn't effective if you cower at the thought of anything but a smile from your workers. I've found that mine actually respect me more because I'm not afraid of them. Like a shark, people can sense fear. If they think you're afraid of them they will take advantage of you to no end. Instead, pretend you are a general leading your troop into battle. Teach and reinforce your battle plans and expectations so they know what to do when you're not leading the charge. I have found that my workers have adapted the "do it right the first time" mentality. Keeping the tough love balanced with praise has truly helped me create a productive, balanced workplace full of respect and passion. Like Steve said, *"Be a yardstick of quality..."*

Heather Sahli is the Founder/CEO of Operation:Warm Winter, Inc. Known for sending 28.6 million blankets to Japan, she's also a philanthropist, writer, and socialite.
For more information, visit www.operationwarmwinterinc.com

"I can live for two months on a good compliment."
Mark Twain

In a few brief words, Twain expressed something profound and far too true.

There are stories we've all heard about people who received a modest compliment but remembered it for years. Sometimes the most casual but genuine remark can have an impact far beyond what one would expect.

Giving a compliment to a co-worker or an employee is one of the most powerful management tools you will ever use. And yet, too few bosses make use of it. It comes back to knowing yourself and being comfortable with who you are. When you forget self and think instead about others, the impact a sincere compliment can have becomes so apparent. More than just brightening someone's day, with a compliment, you are recognizing a positive, encouraging more of that same action and giving sustenance to an employees' soul.

To add more impact to your comment, be sure to include specifics. If someone handled a complaint call well, make mention of the fine method they used. If an employee finished a job in record time, cite the speed and efficiency. Giving specifics make the compliment more meaningful and helps the worker to understand what action is desired to be repeated.

To a large degree, you cannot overdo praise. However, if it is flippant, too casual, undeserving or insincere, then you will have damaged your own credibility. This will impede your progress as a manager and make hollow all past and future remarks. So, seek out excellence and compliment it wherever you find it but be sure to be truthful, honest and genuine at all times.

"I have yet to find a man, however exalted his station, who did not do better work and put forth greater effort under a spirit of approval than under a spirit of criticism."
Charles M. Schwab

Following up on Twain is Schwab's cherry on the top. For all laws seem to have a corollary. And the pleasant side effect of giving praise when deserved is the aftermath of that effusive action.

Think about your own efforts under others. Did you not try harder to please after being praised the first time? And did you not have confidence that you could do it again?

If you are a manager today, you have no doubt experienced that rush of pride and confidence that you get from having performed well. And when someone we admire (or answer to) notes those efforts and takes the time to acknowledge them, we all respond similarly.

Given that your goal as a manager is to achieve your desired results, imagine the cost of missing the opportunity to give an employee a confidence boost. Imagine how much more effective you would be if all your employees were trying hard to improve on their last effort.

Instill that spirit of approval. When being critical, select your words carefully. Giving a compliment on effort coupled with a suggestion for improvement is far more effective than a harsh rebuke. Always allow the employee to preserve their dignity as you guide them to greater performance.

Motivation to do better truly comes from within, but it is nurtured and sustained by outside influences.

"Commitment is the enemy of resistance, for it is the serious promise to press on, to get up, no matter how many times you are knocked down."

David McNally

There is a scene in the movie Rocky that has touched many a heart. More so for those who have struggled uphill against formidable odds.

It occurred in the fight scene at the end: A low-level boxer, Rocky, faces Apollo Creed, the Heavyweight Champion of the World. And as Rocky made clear in a previous scene, *"...all I wanna do is go the distance. Nobody's ever gone the distance with Creed. And if I can go that distance and that bell rings and I'm still standin', I'm gonna know for the first time in my life, see, that I weren't just another bum from the neighborhood."*

Rocky is getting hammered all fight long. Pundits forecasted it would be a short three round cakewalk for the Champ. But late in the fight, Rocky is still standing. Near the end, Apollo knocks Rocky down for the fourth or fifth time and retreats to his corner expecting victory. But, of course, Rocky gets back up again and, staring at Apollo through bloody eyes, he signals with his outstretched gloves that he is ready for more. He waves Apollo towards him and it is in that moment that he defines commitment.

Find your mission and commit to it. Not just in words but in thought, deed and a relentless spirit. Being knocked to the canvass is just another chance to show how fast you can get back up again. There is no force as powerful as the serious promise to press on.

MAKING IT EASIER TO SUCCEED
As told by Barry Maher

I once took a position as a sales manager with a Fortune 100 company, with the understanding that my unit had been first in sales in the division the year before. However when I got there, I found that the six person unit had three rookies and had just lost the region's top salesperson via transfer. Now my unit was dead last in the region and deep in a hole.

Morale would have had to improve greatly to reach abominable. The new division manager was immediately disliked, and everything she tried seemed to make the problem worse. She scattered candy dishes around an office where most of the employees were trying to diet. She pumped in unpopular Muzak. Her idea of "motivation" left vets amused and rookies confused.

Sales people need a strong sense of confidence, so in my first meeting with my new unit, I told them that within one year they were going to be number one in Sales. Within less than a year they were exactly that. So how did I build their morale and turn the unit around. I didn't. They did. I just made it possible for them to do it.

1) I demonstrated faith in them. To me, great leadership is about showing your people that there is more in them than they know: I showed them that I truly believed they had the capability to be the best. Then I acted as if that were true. In return, they tried to live up to my expectations. Eventually, they adopted those expectations as their own and aimed to fill them.

2) I demonstrated my loyalty to them. I fought for them and championed them in the division and in the company. I had their best interests at heart. I found out what their short term and long term goals were, and together we worked out concrete plans for reaching those goals.

3) I explained my belief that the company was a selling organization and that they were the most important

people in the company. I told them that all the rest of us, the administrators, the managers, the VPs, the CEO, were sales support.

4) I praised and rewarded them for their accomplishments and made sure the company did too.

5) Together, we created a team mentality. We set up a mentoring program that went beyond the constant training that I was doing. No one who wanted or needed help was ever left alone with a problem.

6) I made it OK to make a mistake, to fail. They learned to review every call, every day, every week and every month, always asking themselves what they could have done better. But after absorbing the lesson, they learned to absolve themselves—leaving the mistakes behind—and move on to the next call.

7) Whenever possible, we turned negatives into positives. For example, we discussed how the top salesperson in any company is always the one who hears the most Noes. We tracked how many Noes we got and learned to deflect them and continue probing. Eventually of course we ended up, also collecting the most Yeses.

8) We had fun. And we made having fun on the job and in the accounts a priority. We tried to create an atmosphere where everyone would look forward to going to work, and look forward to making the calls. A salesperson who enjoys what he is doing will sell more. One who can make the call fun for the prospect is half way to a sale.

Barry Maher is a Principle at Barry Maher & Associates in Corona, CA. Barry helps companies turn their sales people into sales superstars. His clients include ABC, AT&T, Blue Cross, Hewlett-Packard, McDonald's, the U.S. Government, Verizon and Wells Fargo, among others. For more information, visit www.barrymaher.com.

"So much of what we call management consists of making it difficult for people to work."

                                               Peter Drucker

Take a few hours and spend them analyzing all the actions and processes that your employees perform each day. Focus particularly on those activities that you have been doing in the same way for years and years. Then ask yourself, is all this really necessary? Why are we really doing it this way and what has changed in our world since we began this process?

Many times you will find that a part of the process is geared to back up systems that are no longer necessary in a digital world. Or you will uncover process steps that are totally outdated or redundant. Sometimes you will discover that you are requiring higher level employees to do something that others could do just as easily. In any event, the world is changing at a faster pace now than ever before and that requires constant reexamination of process and procedures.

Or, there is an easier way to identify what you are doing that is making work more difficult. Ask your employees. Or have someone ask them for you. In either case, tell them the company wants to streamline processes and make them simpler. Just ask them what they do that is unnecessary and too time consuming for the value gained. What they tell you will be mostly true and that which is not, presents a great opportunity to explain to them why.

When you have open communication with your people, together you can eliminate unproductive tasks and gain the intangible benefits of a spirit of cooperation.

"In this economy, there are two kinds of business managers: those who are humble and those who soon will be."
Gary Brose

This is a paraphrase from a quote uttered by a forlorn baseball manager who admitted his humility came from experience.

Life can be a hard teacher. Often in life, circumstances have more of an effect on outcomes than personal effort. Recognizing that, to some extent, we are all along for the ride can unburden a leader.

Ever had a boss who was a braggart and know-it-all? Someone who claimed to have never failed and had a virtual birthright to leadership? Did you see what happened when something went wrong? We have all been there. In that situation, the infallible leader always blames it on someone else. There is always a scapegoat or a villain that has victimized him. Why? Because that is his only defense. He can't admit that he is as mortal as you. And, in the end, that type of manager fails.

For those of you who have adopted some form of the 'infallible leader' management style, it is not too late to ease off and show a more humble side. If you are just starting out in management and still finding your voice, be humble and do good work. Others will sing your praises for you and their song will be sweeter than anything you could croon.

Being a humble manager, one who admits her own errors and gives credit to others removes the yoke of perfection off of her own shoulders. Her employees will help to carry the load and they will work far more collaboratively to reach the company goals. The choice is yours: Be humble now and gain the immediate advantages or inevitably be humbled later and lose all credibility and power.

>"We made too many wrong mistakes."
>Yogi Berra

The master of the malapropism, Yogi Berra was actually a very astute baseball manager. His comments often sounded inane but the truth to them was always evident.

In the above quote, Yogi was discussing a game the Yankees had lost and describing the course of events. There was a simple yet elegant business lesson in his words. He did not dodge responsibility. He did not claim that his team was a victim of untoward circumstances. He just admitted that they had failed. *"We made too many wrong mistakes."* OK, even if they had been right mistakes, we all get the idea.

In business, taking a clear, matter-of-fact approach to analyzing your own failures can reap great rewards. Couple that approach with a healthy dose of humility and you have a formula for identifying the underlying causes. In Yogi's case, player fundamentals were weak and that weakness was exposed and exploited by the other team. The corrective action was to spend more time on basics: Hitting the cutoff man, throwing to the correct base, backing up the catcher at the right time. All these things were worked on in subsequent weeks and were improved overall.

When you admit your failures head on, you open the door to new ideas and the true discovery of the factors that led to the problem in the first place. When you point blame on others or sidestep responsibility, you bury the problem until it comes back later with a vengeance.

Learn from Yogi. Admit your errors and move on.

"Surround yourself with the best people you can find, delegate authority, and don't interfere as long as the policy you've decided upon is being carried out."

Ronald Reagan

Delegation, decentralization, releasing authority and empowering others are probably the most challenging aspects of being an effective manager. It is not easily done and, certainly, is something that takes a modest leap of faith.

The trick is to do it one small baby step at a time. Delegating responsibility requires a belief in a subordinate's abilities and a maturity of leadership. It means that you, as manager, must communicate clearly what your objectives are and both parties must fully understand and be on the same page. It also requires a leap of faith on your part and a strong sense of responsibility on the others'.

Is it possible to succeed without delegating and empowering others? Absolutely! A small business owner can run her business effectively by controlling virtually every important aspect of the business herself. But, at some point, greater growth becomes impossible. Long term growth and success can only be achieved by working through others. And that can only be done with delegation. Of course, no one said anything about delegating duties and then walking away. A key to successful delegation is frequent review and follow-up. Getting regular updates on progress is mandatory. That gives the manager the opportunity for course corrections and modest changes to insure that the objectives you communicated are being adhered to. Suddenly, delegation isn't as scary anymore. Dole out the responsibility a little at a time and keep close tabs. Be like Ronnie. You'll like it.

"The best executive is the one who has sense enough to pick good men to do what he wants done, and self-restraint to keep from meddling with them while they do it."

Theodore Roosevelt

So this makes two presidents we quote about delegation and empowerment. Seeing a trend? Clearly, those who have achieved the highest positions have learned how to function in a world where they do not try to micro-manage and control everything.

Many managers have lamented after delegating a specific project, that they should have done it themselves. They find no peace in allowing others to do it when the final result is not exactly as they hoped. They are micro-managers who yearn for the personal satisfaction of doing it 'their way'.

With every delegation, there is a trade off. As a manager, you have to come to grips with the value of that trade-off. Many are unable to do this and it is in that moment that they doom themselves to always being a lower level manager or business owner of a small enterprise.

The trade off is simple. Inevitably, whomever you delegate some task to, will do it in his own unique way and the result may not be exactly as you wanted. A mature manager recognizes that and accepts that the value lies not in the end product of what the subordinate achieves but in the time that they create for you to do something more impactful. After delegating a task that you used to do, the onus falls upon you to maximize your extra time to do something far more important. If you cannot do that, the failure is yours not theirs.

Emulate Teddy. Delegate, follow up but avoid meddling and move on to bigger and better things.

THE MICRO-MANAGED EMPLOYEE'S LAMENT

From a November 18th, 2011 submission on the website www.stop-micro-management.com

You are about to get an ear full – I need to vent. At this moment I am sitting on the floor of my apartment crying and basically having a pseudo panic attack.
I'm in sales, I have been for six years and I am a damn good sales person. Unfortunately, every manager I've had has been either psychotic, micro managing or both. I never think a boss could be worse than the current one but I am always surprised and proven wrong. I am currently in sales for a corporate company that is "supposed" to be like owning your own business – yeah, my ass.
There were two managers I interviewed with – I was told it was a toss-up on who I'd answer to after starting. One of them was freaking awesome and the other was very tall, overweight and thought he was the coolest person ever.
I can spot a micromanaging a-hole from a mile away, but at this point I was out of options and simply had to take the job. So I did. And prayed, prayed hard that I would get to work for the cool manager.
Of course – that didn't happen. I will give it to him that he is definitely getting micro managed from the top (how much so, I don't know).
I'm just going to list in bullets.
• on a sales call ride along – rude to customers, doesn't listen, talks a lot and fast, taps his leg like he is on crack, and basically ruins the sales call.
• in field for maybe a year or two and promoted.
• the absolute most arrogant person I have ever met.
• doesn't read emails.
• used to sell cars.
• I have all but stopped emailing or calling him to ask questions, because he doesn't answer the question; yells when replying and he usually throws in an insult for me not already knowing the answer.
• every night I am required to send him a report of everything I did that day and the sales that I have made.
• when I haven't made any sales -I'm not typically very happy about it. You can bet your bippy to expect an a-hole response citing at least one thing that you are doing "wrong". All replies consist of exclamation points.

I can never do enough, do anything right. I know that it is a sin to hate someone, but I am very close. He makes my life absolutely miserable and I feel so trapped and helpless.

In spring 2010 I left a job I'd been at for one year. I was doing well, but was working for yet another psychotic micromanager (reeked of smoke, on pain pills. I could say more but need to be discreet). The company was crazy but the big boss loved me and believed in me. Looking back, I always had that to fall back on. But I was wined and dined away to join a new company.

That one was a complete nightmare as well and ended with me getting on unemployment where I stayed for the maximum term of seven months. The best freaking time of my life. I vowed to not take another job that would put so much pressure on me ever again. I took my time, truly sought other options, but I finally ran out of time – I had no choice but to take this job.

Now I've been here for nine months (I know this because my boss has told me three times this week that after nine months I should know the answers to the questions I'm asking or be able to get things done quicker). So in the past say, five years I have worked for six different employers.

I swear to all that I am not a bad employee. I know that it likely seems that way. But I am enthusiastic, optimistic and actually like what I do. I'm talented and have proven it.

But it's never good enough to just mute him. He has gotten under my skin. The heat is on and I am helpless. Writing this was helpful. I have no idea if you will even read it. But feel free to post. Even if I don't hear back from you, I may still write again with updates.

As I've written this, I've realized that no one has the right to ruin my morale like this. I don't know what I am going to do – but I know that quitting isn't an option right now – so it's time for war.

This could get interesting. Thanks for creating this site, not sure if it is designed to be a place for ones to vent, but I just made it one for me!

Peace :)

This email is from one of my readers, "Perpetually Micro-Managed."
A very emotional personal story, it is published here on my site with a kind permission of the author. Many of us are in the same or similar situation, unfortunately. I created my website, www.stop-micro-management.com for you, micromanaged and mistreated hardworking and dedicated employees.
For more information, stop by and add your thoughts.
A., the Webmaster

"**Few things help an individual more than to place responsibility upon him, and to let him know that you trust him.**"

        Booker T. Washington

  The power of true delegation continues to be a common thread in a manager's quest to create a positive work environment. This is the other side of delegation. This is about what delegation implies. Stated simply, when you delegate, you are saying to one of your employees that you trust them. The power of that should not go unmentioned.

  Successful delegation begins at the first meeting. And being a strong communicator is a mandatory arrow in any manager's quiver. The seeds of success or failure of a single delegated duty are planted at that first meeting.

  When you meet with your employee to discuss the delegated duty, be prepared and be thorough. Be sure to explain why you are choosing to delegate this now. Talk about why she has been handpicked by you as the person to do this task. Discuss how you want it done and describe in detail what the finished product should look like. Prepare well for this meeting and do not minimize its importance. Finally, settle on a specific schedule for update meetings at which your employee will report progress to you.

  And then do the one thing that must be done to seal the deal. Look your employee in the eye and tell them in no uncertain terms that you are counting on them and that you trust them and believe in them. And if you can't do that with sincerity, then find someone else for the job.

  Mr. Washington was an insightful man. Bestowing that trust and responsibility is a compliment of the highest order. Make sure your employee sees it that way too.

"The single biggest problem in communication is the illusion that it has taken place."

George Bernard Shaw

How many times have you cried in exasperation *"But we just talked about that yesterday!"*

It is a frequent refrain in business (and in life in general) and we have heard it all before. And yet, it continues to plague us. And not just in the spoken word ... it occurs in the written word constantly.

In today's world we are competing with a never ending barrage of verbal and visual stimuli that demands our attention and our retention. In the business world this problem is magnified and intensified. In business, failure to retain information can cost a company serious money and can even lead to total failure. Much is at stake.

So what is the solution? Listen better? Try harder? Speak louder? Write clearer? Thanks a lot. Those aren't solutions. Those are bromides.

Look more closely at what Shaw is saying. He states that the problem is the **illusion** that communication took place. Ah, there is the rub. And there is the attack point for all managers.

Do not assume that communication has taken place. Even when you know it has. Assume instead, that someone, somewhere, did not really get it and it is that person who will mess up the works. Then re-attack the communication conundrum.

Re-communicate. Emphasize the most important points in memos by bolding them up or using a different color. Post notices where appropriate. Ask people if they can tell you the key points of the policy at issue. Reinforce all that you have said before until you are satisfied that the significant issues are understood by all. Fight the illusion.

"When people talk, listen completely. Most people never listen."

Ernest Hemingway

What do you do when locked in an intense conversation with a co-worker debating the right process to solve a problem? Do you listen to her every word and contemplate the deeper meanings of what she is saying?

Or do you do as most of us do? Spend your time formulating your rebuttal and waiting for her to finish?

Particularly, in business, you will have many conversations of this sort. Perhaps in a review as an employee is disagreeing with your analysis of their performance, you will allow them to voice their thoughts. Do you actually listen to what they are saying and give it due consideration? Or are you busy preparing your counter-attack so that you can keep control of the conversation and defend your position?

A perceptive comment on this was once delivered by Fran Drescher in her role as Fran Lebowitz, The Nanny on TV. Locked in a heated exchange with a co-star, Fran said, *"The opposite of talking is not listening. The opposite of talking is waiting."* Too true for too many of us.

Fran wasn't listening at all. She was just waiting for the other person to stop talking so she could unload her next barrage. We laughed when we heard that line because we knew how true it was.

Here is a good thought. In every conversation, listen intently as though the person you were talking to were the world's expert on that topic. When you do that, you would naturally give value to their words. If, after that, you can still counter with a cogent point, then your response will have more validity and ring more true.

Be a good listener and, in turn, when you speak others will listen with open minds.

THE FRAME GAME
By Amy Carroll

As we communicate with each other, human beings construct different frames. Frames are like the mood, tone, atmosphere, environment or ambience of an interaction. Frames can be positive (friendly, playful, respectful, energizing, for example) or negative (tense, angry, disrespectful, bored). We set frames through our body language, voice and the words we use.

Unconsciously, we are constantly setting frames and being invited into others' frames. The danger is, that when we're not aware of another person's frame, we can get caught in it like a trap. Positive frames are not usually a concern. It's when we get caught in others' negative frames that can cause problems.

In my consulting career, I have observed many instances of negative frame interactions. They tend to go something like this:

Imagine Jeff enters Chris's office and says *"Chris, I asked you to get me the layout for the client pitch we've got this afternoon. It's already 2pm and I don't have it yet!",* speaking with an annoyed, slightly aggressive and sarcastic tone.

Chris hears the words. He also hears the tone and the unspoken "idiot" at the end of the sentence. Getting immediately triggered, Chris matches his semi muffled, antagonistic tone and says: *"Well Jeff, if you were paying attention in the team meeting yesterday, you would have heard me tell you I was putting the layout in the client file for you to review this morning!"*

Now Chris is pleased because he got to turn it back on Jeff. In fact, he has one-upped Jeff with concrete evidence of his apparent lack of intelligence. The problem is, as a result of this exchange their relationship has been slightly damaged. It will take time and effort to repair or it may get worse. Either way there is a potential cost in energy and time (money) and could possibly spill over into the client meeting later that day causing further problems.

So imagine the same interaction after a little coaching where Chris learns the power to avoid others' negative frames and instead setting a more positive frame. Let's rewind the scene with that in mind:

Jeff walks into Chris's office. *"Chris, I asked you to get me the layout for the client pitch we've got this afternoon. It's already 2pm and I don't have it yet!",* speaking with the same annoyed, slightly aggressive and sarcastic tone.

Chris hears the message and just before he instinctively reacts, he remembers to pause, take a deep breath, put his ego to the side and chooses to respond by saying:

"You probably didn't hear me yesterday at the meeting when I mentioned that I was putting it in the client file for you to review. You'll find it there." (Chris' voice is relaxed and upbeat).

Like many people, Jeff is an intelligent guy. He knows that if he keeps using a nasty tone, he's going to start looking stupid pretty quickly. Instead, he responds in a more positive, respectful way with something like, *"Great thanks. See you at the meeting at 3."* Because Chris was aware of Jeff's negative frame, put his ego to the side, resisted the temptation to react, which helped Jeff "save face", Jeff's behavior has been positively shifted and potential conflict averted. Plus Jeff is less likely to respond aggressively in the future with Chris because he didn't get the reaction he was expecting.

Listening and truly hearing the other person in the conversation can make everyone more at ease and more effective. So, listen, pause, think and then respond. Life will be easier.

Amy Carroll, owner of Carroll Communication Coaching, is a Swiss-based coach, trainer and speaker. She specializes in leadership, communication and effectiveness training for multinational clients with global objectives and teams. For more information, visit www.carrollcoaching.com.

"Mystification is simple; clarity is the hardest thing of all."
Julian Barnes

So we continue harping on communication. Why is communication so important to creating the right work atmosphere? Most managers know it is because it is central to all elements of work and life.

Barnes says that clarity is the hardest thing of all. Think about some of the lessons learned in life. If you boil them down, they tend to move in the direction of simplicity. And simple things are the clearest of all.

When a business problem is analyzed with the intent of finding out how or why it happened, the answer is almost invariably 'poor communication'. Somewhere along the line, one person did not get the memo. Or somebody missed a meeting. Or an employee wasn't paying attention. Or everyone failed to listen. And what we have here, as Strother Martin exclaimed in Cool Hand Luke *"…is a failure to communicate."*

But honestly, it is more than that. It is a failure to simplify. It is a failure to achieve clarity. People remember and understand concepts expressed clearly. It is easy to satisfy your desire to communicate by proceeding to obfuscate and mystify in a four page memo outlining all the steps that must be taken to address a specific issue. It is much harder to simplify it and write it in short paragraphs so that it is understood and retained. Those who can clarify have power.

Some companies have found that a simple universal rule resolves that issue. For example, "Safety first, then go ahead." or "Solve the customer's problem, everything else is secondary." is the kind of directive that can guide your employees to make the right choices even when they are not sure of exact proper procedure.

Demystify and strive for clarity. Life will be simpler.

"How very little can be done under the spirit of fear."
Florence Nightingale

Florence Nightingale lived in the mid 1800's during troubled times. She survived the terrors of the Crimean War so she probably knew something more about fear than we do in our daily business lives.

Her observation, however, is still valid in today's world. Even in the business world. How many times have you witnessed a co-worker shirking responsibility because he was fearful of failing? How often have you seen an employee dodge a confrontation with a wrong-doer because she didn't want to be involved? This occurs many times at every business every day of the week.

Why? Because the employee perceives that the downside to action is far greater than the upside. And the fear of failure in any form, makes even the effort unappealing.

As a manager, you must decrease that fear: By your actions, by your deeds, by your attitude. Make the failure to try more unattractive than the failure to succeed. When someone does fail, discuss it openly with them and with others, clearly indicating what was learned from it and giving credit to the employee who tried. Praise the willingness to tackle difficult issues regardless of the outcome. Honor those who step up and try; not just those who succeed. With the concept of 'All things in moderation' in mind, you would not want to encourage reckless, costly or ill-advised attempts, of course.

To create an atmosphere that encourages action, decrease the perceived penalty for failure while still using the opportunity to make it a constructive teaching moment. You want to develop a cadre of fearless action takers, not shirkers and dodgers. Remember that the next time someone tries but comes up short.

"The fear of being wrong is the prime inhibitor of the creative process."

Jean Bryant

There is another byproduct of fear that is succinctly summarized here by Jean Bryant.

Whether you are an architect designing a new building or a grocery store stocker loading up shelves, the creative urge is truly affected by fear: the fear of criticism, the fear of failure and the fear of fragile job security. The architect may have a unique and controversial design in mind but she has been stung by criticism before and is not anxious to revisit that feeling. The stocker may have an idea for a different concept in product placement but he avoids bringing it up because his boss isn't open to innovative notions.

When people are not afraid, the creative juices flow more freely. Without the creative process, no progress is made. Purposely minimizing that creativity sets you up as the only one left to affect change. Think how much more effective your business could be if everyone felt they could dream up ideas and be sure they would be heard.

As a manager, you can show that you are always open to discussion. Perhaps your employees' ideas are faulty but if only one out of ten is adopted, you would be further ahead than you are now. Make it clear you want to hear any wacky or off-the-wall idea that someone comes up with. At some point, someone's idea will be brilliant or it will create conversation that leads to a more practical refinement of the suggestion.

Either way, you are engaging and involving your people and, at the very least, having a good laugh. Together. As a team. Making the job of the day to day business more of a quixotic journey helps people stay motivated, amused and occupied.

"Comedy is simply a funny way of being serious."
Peter Ustinov

A wonderfully under-valued element to creating the right atmosphere for maximum motivation is the use of humor. And as Peter Ustinov so cleverly put it, comedy makes us laugh because it twists the truth in a funny way. Much can be accomplished with humor that cannot be done in any other way.

If you are a manager with a great sense of humor or comedic timing, use it to maximum advantage. Learn about your employees and figure out what they think is funny, then share a laugh with them. Everyone certainly is different and needs to be treated with care but you can tailor your humor to get your points across with the right level of levity.

If you are not necessarily a gifted comedian and have a hard time joking around, good advice is to try a few baby steps here and there. Build up your confidence one short one-liner at a time. When workers on the job can laugh together it develops a bond and camaraderie that you don't get otherwise.

Obviously, all humor must be appropriate and never off-color. But, it truly is different between men and women. With many men, it is possible to praise them in a humorous way by saying something like *"For an extremely ugly fellow, Jake certainly does a good job in sales."* For some odd reason, guys respond well to being called ugly. Probably not a good approach with your female employees, so tailor your humor accordingly.

And finally, self-deprecating humor is a true winner for managers. Making fun of yourself puts people at ease and helps the work atmosphere stay loose. Try it when you can but always be sure to tread carefully.

WE CAN ALL DARE TO BE SUPERHEROES

John Scholl, a Seattle entrepreneur has a Graphics and Printing business called BIGink and one of his key goals is to create an outstanding working environment both physically and mentally. I visited John's office/warehouse and was amazed by what I saw. John is a very hands-on manager and is very involved in his company. He knows how to create images that sell and he used that knowledge to create an incredibly unique office space for his employees.

John moved into an 18,000 square foot building in an industrial area just south of Downtown Seattle. The office was not much to look at and it was painted a dreary gray. John wanted to paint the outside of the building to make it stand out so he spent $30,000 to paint it blue and yellow in an eye catching motif. The company name is in big letters on the side and front of the building. Now, you should know, this is in an area of town not known for color splashes or eye-catching displays. But John felt that the employees needed to be proud of where they worked and the customers needed to be impressed that John practiced what he preached.

But as impressive as the outside was, the inside just blew me away. All the walls were painted in colorful fashion and there were standup cutouts of life-size Superhero characters everywhere! On walls in every room, you would see cutouts of The Flash, AquaMan, Green Lantern and many others. Each employee adopted one Superhero to be their alter ego and it served as a constant reminder that they were expected to do super feats of wonder in their daily job. Smaller cutouts of those same characters marked their place in the rankings for the top sales reps on the monthly chart and sayings printed on the wall were daily affirmations that greatness is possible even in a small Seattle printing company.

And there was more. The crew had developed an affinity for English rock bands of the 60's, 70's and 80's. There were more cardboard cutouts and posters of the Stones, the Beatles, The Who, Elvis Costello and many others. OK, this was a FUN place to work! Music played in the background and the entire environment seemed to cry out "Let's have some fun here"!

Is there more to creating a positive work environment? Of course, there is. But what John had done was to create a setting that said that he cared about his people; that he believed in their super abilities and that he was confident that if they could have fun and enjoy themselves, their work product would be better and stronger. And, he put his money where his mouth (and heart) was. What he built was and is a fantastic starting point and a super springboard for greater success.

John Scholl is the President and owner of BIGink Printing in Seattle. He has been in the print industry for over 30 years and has unique insights into human nature and the science of motivation.

SUMMARY:

Creating the right business atmosphere is the single most important step you can take in motivating your staff. All other initiatives spring from your business ambiance so pay particular attention to your efforts here.

Be sure to:
- Know yourself and be yourself. Use your particular character strengths to tailor your efforts to create a truly motivational environment. And remember, genuineness builds; insincerity destroys.
- Praise appropriately and often. Criticize gently and constructively. Giving frequent recognition engenders subsequent correct behavior.
- Commit wholeheartedly to fashioning a business atmosphere that encourages independent thought, action and participation.
- Be sincerely humble and remove the pressure to be perfect. Admit your mistakes or failures and set an example so that others see there is a taste of glory not just in the winning, but in the trying.
- Develop your skills at delegation. Tune up your ability to trust others and work through others for those who delegate effectively have no ceiling.
- Open your ears and curb your tongue. Truly listen to people and search for honesty and truth. Be frugal with your speech. Cultivate a more serene and calm demeanor. People will not remember a thousand word diatribe but they will hang on your every word when your utterances are succinct, lucid and insightful.

By creating the right atmosphere, you are setting the stage for everything that follows. Being accessible, open to discourse, and viewed as a positive manager creates an optimum environment that will allow you to succeed at all other steps, including those first crucial strides in building your team: Hiring the right people.

CHAPTER THREE

HIRE THE RIGHT PEOPLE

"Get the right people on the bus and in the right seat."
Jim Collins

The author of the book, "Good to Great", Jim Collins researched dozens of companies that rose from being a serious player in their industry to being the #1 powerhouse for an extended period of time. He searched for the common denominators of success and concluded that a very key element of success was high quality hiring.

Many of us have grown up to believe that companies with a shrewd and dynamic vision have risen to the top simply because they have 'built a better mousetrap'. But Collins research proved that thought to be false. Business history is littered with examples of companies that had the best product but failed to rise to a position of prominence in their industry.

Instead, what he learned is that those companies that succeeded reached the top because they had high quality employees in all the key positions. Simply put, they hired the right people and all of them were in the correct seats on the company bus. As Collins also said, *"People are not your most important asset. The right people are."*

Now look at your company or your department. Do you have the right people? Are they all in the role they are most suited for? Is someone filling a slot because you are not sure what else to do with him? Is one employee slowing everyone else down because she can't keep up? Greatness is not achieved by mediocre employees or good workers in the wrong roles. Your job is to put the right people in the right seats. Do it now.

"If you pick the right people and give them the opportunity to spread their wings – and put compensation as a carrier behind it – you almost don't have to manage them."
                                        Jack Welch

Notice that Jack Welch's sentence starts with an IF. He is reiterating what Collins said. Moving your business forward starts with the assumption that you already have all the right people in the right places. That remains as the number one priority.

When interviewing and hiring, it pays to be as diligent as you would be if you were buying a $50,000 or $100,000 piece of equipment. After all, that may be what the new hire costs you before you realize if he was the right one to hire in the first place. A great way to protect yourself and make better selections is to take advantage of services that can help you identify applicants' capabilities and temperament. A company such as Profiles International is a leader in that field and a good place to start.

Once they are all there, you, as manager, need to provide the proper incentives. Recognizing that everyone is different and each employee responds to different stimuli when it comes to motivation, it is still possible to focus on the basic motivational prodding irons.

Some people respond best to good old-fashioned monetary stimuli. When done correctly, rewarding good work with higher pay or bonuses can be very effective. Others react to recognition and praise. To those, offer a generous dose of both with sincerity and honesty as deserved. Still others respond to more ethereal motivations: a highly moral goal or a result that benefits others.

In any case, when you find the trigger that motivates each employee or the group of workers, employ it and maximize it. A team of dedicated, inspired and super-charged employees will manage themselves and strive for greatness whether you are watching over their shoulder or not.

"The way a team plays as a whole determines its success. You may have the greatest bunch of individual stars in the world, but if they don't play together, the club won't be worth a dime."

Babe Ruth

The legendary, larger than life Babe Ruth was probably as close to a one-man team as there ever will be. In 1921, he hit 59 homeruns, a personal total greater than most every team in the American League. If ever a man had a right to say that his teammates were unimportant, it was the Babe.

But he didn't say that. Ruth recognized that a team's success is more likely when the teammates complement each other and function together as one. He knew that there were intangibles at work here. That a 'happy clubhouse' always seemed to win more games and enjoy the season's journey more.

Part of the challenge of hiring the right people is to find talent that will fit in and mesh well with your current personnel. And part of being able to do that is to make sure that your current employees are already the right ones. If half your staff are in the 'wrong seats on the bus' or are simply not the best workers, you need to resolve that issue first. You can't be hiring people so that they will fit in with those who are the wrong people on the bus. Hire to replace those people and when you get everyone in the right seat, hire to complement them.

And every now and then, hire the sparkplug who will shake things up and reenergize your company ...

DIVERSITY IN THE EMPLOYEE GENE POOL
As told by Greg Kidd

Sometimes, opportunities present themselves in the strangest ways. Two of my most fortuitous hires occurred in the least likely way.

In the mid 1980's I was in New Zealand working on assignments with a number of former state owned enterprises that were deregulating based on Thatcher principles of free markets. The NZ banking industry was ahead of its time and had eliminated float by using couriers to move all the checks same day to processing facilities so that they could clear overnight. The dispatch process was executed using little paper tickets – and that looked like an opportunity for computerization.

By this time, I already had a programmer in hand by the name of Erik Westra. He had responded to an ad I placed looking for a graphic artist that could take numbers from a new software product called Excel and turn them into pretty pictures. I had hired him for the equivalent of about US $5 an hour from a bulletin board ad at the local university. He hadn't used any of the programs before, but was an astonishing learner and put my modeling work to shame within a week. He looked at everything with "beginner's eyes" to comprehend its fundamental potential, and then zoomed by experienced users once he grasped the essence of the possible. But his real magic was in writing visualization code. He modeled the entire NZ check clearing system so that we could reduce the number of centers from 13 to 3 by more efficiently utilizing courier networks. I could literally watch the couriers and checks move through the road arteries of the country to arrive just-in-time at processing centers that converted all that paper into electronic credits and debits.

The software Erik created was then used to run local courier firms in Wellington. Successes there lead to a spread in usage through the country and then to the west coast of the U.S. Three years later we raised $70M on the Nasdaq and purchased many of our users – integrating 62 companies across Australia, Asia, North America and Europe in a year's time. All that software to run the network was created by one local hire from a University job board.

About this time I was contacted by yet another student named Jack. He informed me that our company's web site had a number of weaknesses that he'd like to point out, and also mentioned that he too had a fascination with dispatch software. His matter of fact spunk impressed me and I made him an offer sight unseen for him to come and live and work with us on our upcoming IPO. It meant dropping out of school, which didn't seem to faze him at all – despite the fact that we didn't even discuss what he'd be paid or his specific duties.

Jack didn't rewrite the software Erik built, but he did critique it all and point out opportunities for us to rethink our foundations. Erik had remained in New Zealand so it was Jack who was on premise when the investment bankers came to do due diligence on our IPO. When I presented them with 20 year old Jack as our most knowledgeable tech person, they asked him what part of the system he knew about as they were expecting to meet other leads after him. He matter-of-factly answered "all of it."

When my company Dispatch Management Services Corp got too stuffy, I quit as Chairman and took just two employees with me (Erik and Jack) out of our workforce of 5,000. People wondered why I would give up so much and take so little. But I always felt I got the better part of the deal. The courier industry has been in cyclical decline ever since its peak years at the end of the 1990s. But the idea of dispatch and clearing and settlement are applicable to many other realms.

Erik continued to work with me, and Jack continued to work and live with me (and even helped with nanny duties when I had my first newborn). As he gained confidence he began to work on some of his own ideas that were now more formed. He'd learned a lot about dispatching to couriers via text messaging. Jack's insight was to realize that you could text out not just jobs, but any piece of information that an individual (not just couriers) might want to follow.

But what could you do with just 140 characters? Well the fact that this idea became Twitter has given us all that answer – a lot! And now with Square, Jack's latest idea for taking, rather than making payments with one's phone, a million small businesses can now take credit cards that would likely never have qualified for a traditional merchant account.

Jack and Erik both had a unique perspective. They shook things up for us. I learned that when assessing talent in the interview process, I am far better off when I pay more attention to a prospect's projected arc than where they are today. Jack and Erik had potential and I was lucky enough to see it. Adding some diversity to the employee gene pool is an effective way to create change and add impetus to new directions. To this day, I look back and remember in awe some of the things that Jack said to me. Jack believed that *'freedom of speech might be truly important but the freedom to listen is actually more transforming and revolutionary.'* He clearly had a different way of looking at life. And with Twitter, it turns out he was right.

That shy introverted Jack that I hired and listened to as he talked about his ideas, grew into the Jack Dorsey who has created two billion dollar companies in the last five years. And he's had a third idea that's keeping Erik and I busy to this day. But that's another story.

> Greg Kidd was a first round investor in Twitter and has served as an advisor for Square and as a Senior Analyst for the Board of Governors of the Federal Reserve.

"We are most effective as a team when we complement each other without embarrassment and disagree without fear."
Unknown

Too often we believe that motivation is the duty and responsibility of the leader. The boss is the one who must inspire and energize us all. It all comes from the top.

Or does it? When you talk with a military veteran who has finished his tour of duty and he says that he is going back for another tour in some war torn country half a globe away, what do you hear as his motivation? Is it because his superior officer inspired him? Is it because of the Commander In Chief's words of encouragement? No, it's almost always because he doesn't want to let down his buddies. It's because he feels a sense of duty to help his friends and be there for them.

Your business team is most effective when YOU are not the key master of motivation. Much motivation can come from co-workers and friends. When you have created a positive working atmosphere where honesty and truth reign rather than office politics, you can nurture the feelings of genuine caring between employees. When dialogue is open and problems are attacked rather than people, discourse is more free and solutions present themselves more rapidly.

People develop stronger, more open relationships with their fellow employees when disagreements are handled calmly and openly; and when praise for good work is given freely because they know that management does the same. When management is frugal with sharing the credit, employees shrink from praising each other because it detracts from their own meager opportunities to gain praise themselves.

Nurture fairness and evenhandedness and encourage open discourse among your people.

> **"In looking for people to hire, you look for three qualities: integrity, intelligence and energy. And if they don't have the first, the other two will kill you."**
>
> Warren Buffet

Spoken like a man who has been there. In high positions where your influence can make or break a company, it is all the more important to hire the right person and to seek a high level of integrity.

It is likely that Warren Buffet doesn't hire anyone other than top executives and those at the top in his organization must have integrity to manage massive resources well. It certainly follows that an individual with low integrity may be tempted to break a few rules to gain advantage for himself. And if he has that intelligence and energy too, it could lead to disastrous results.

So, this rule must apply only to those at the top, right? Not exactly. When confronted with temptation, could a worker in your lowest position with little integrity damage your company and your reputation? Of course he could.

Buffet's point is an important one. Sometimes, interviewing and hiring can be nothing much more than a crapshoot. Even with background checks, you can never be sure whether your applicant has high moral standards or is simply putting forward a good face. Experience will help you make the right decisions but a post-hiring watchful eye will help confirm your choice. Life is full of small modest tests of character. Watch for those and, whenever possible, gradually give power to those who show the level of integrity that you demand.

BRASHNESS HAS ITS PLACE

Christos had just dropped out of UCLA Graduate School. As a young man who had seen combat as a Fireteam Leader with the 101st Airborne Infantry in Vietnam, he was still learning how to cope and survive in both life and in the business world. Having just moved to Los Angeles in 1973 and in search of work, he saw an ad in the Los Angeles Times with a new airline that was hiring delivery drivers, sales representatives and managers. He responded to the ad, and discovered that the interview would be taking place at a nearby hotel.

Christos' interview was cancelled – he arrived four hours late. But that wouldn't stop him. He looked for the concierge and paid him five dollars to find out the name and room number of the person conducting the interviews. The concierge did, and Christos knocked on the door of the VP of Operations and managed to convince him to conduct the interview – with the door barely cracked and the security chain still on! The VP was so impressed with his *chutzpa*, he told Christos to meet him downstairs at the bar so they could chat about the position.

Unlike the other clean-cut candidates in suits and ties, Christos wore a T-shirt, jeans, sneakers and shoulder-length hair to the interview. He and the VP chatted for over an hour. When the VP asked him which position he was applying for, Christos said "I will do all three for half the price." Despite being impressed by his eagerness and proposition, the VP could only offer him a courier/sales rep position, but was concerned about Christos' lack of knowledge of the L.A. area, given he had just moved there. So he asked Christos "Do you know the area well enough to deliver truckloads of time-sensitive packages while making customer calls, all in a short period of time?"

Christos answered this question with one of his own, *"Can you read a map?"* Taken aback by the brash Vietnam veteran's response, the VP stared at him for a second and then replied, *"Of course."* To which Christos said, *"So can I."*

It was brash, brazen and a bit of irreverent confidence and candidness. Christos and the VP both smiled, had a good laugh, and Christos was given an employment application for what the VP called a once-in-a-lifetime opportunity. Christos showed up for work without even being hired. Two weeks later, he was offered the job but not before having to convince the regional manager that he already had it.

> Dr. Christos M. Cotsakos (with an Honors Ph.D. in Economics from the University of London) began his professional career as a temporary cargo-handler and courier at FedEx and rose through the ranks to become an Account Executive, Station Manager, Regional Manager, Managing Director, VP of the Western Region, and finally, one of the youngest officers at FedEx as the VP and General Manager in charge of Europe, Africa and the Middle East. Dr. Cotsakos went on to become the Chairman & CEO of E*TRADE Group, Inc. and is considered to be one of the visionaries, architects, and entrepreneurs of e-commerce and e-finance.

> "We promote family values here almost as often as we promote family members."
>
> Larry Kersten

Too silly? Too tongue in cheek for you? Take a moment and ask yourself how many companies you have worked at that employed their own family members.

How did that work out? Were they universally liked and appreciated or were they the subject of private behind-the-back jokes? Did you ever sense discord and resentment among the employees over some undeserved promotion given to a family member?

Once again, virtually everyone has a nepotism story to share if you ask them. Rarely do these stories have happy endings. If you are a business owner, think twice and three times before forever altering your team chemistry by employing a relative. And if you do so anyway, do your utmost to treat that relative the same as your other employees ... with no exceptions. As a manager, if you find yourself in the predicament of supervising a family member, there are two courses of action you can take.

You can have a frank and open conversation with ownership to determine if the family member you will be managing will be held to the same standards that everyone else is. And if you come out of that meeting feeling that they truly will, then you are probably deluding yourself. You can make the best of a bad situation and try to continue creating an even playing field and a positive work atmosphere for all, or you can select the second course of action.

Option #2 is to simply vote with your feet. Your chance for success within a company that has one set of standards for a family member and another for everyone else, lies on the far end between slim and none. Life is short. If you are committed to making something great happen in your business life, seek a new opportunity to do well at a different company.

"If I had eight hours to chop down a tree, I'd spend six sharpening my axe."

Abraham Lincoln

Lincoln had natural story telling skills and even in a short sentence he painted a picture so clear that no one could misunderstand it. And he said it so much more colorfully than most of us would.

Preparation has gotten a bad reputation in this fast paced world of ours. It's perceived to take too long and produce so little that it feels unproductive and wasteful. Consequently, most managers' idea of preparation is to catch their breath in the elevator and collect their thoughts on the way up to the next meeting or event. Abe had a different perspective and it would be wise not to discount a man of his standing.

Simply taking time to jot notes on paper about the salient points of discussion before every meeting is a helpful preparation technique. How many times have you been in a meeting, getting caught up in the flow of discourse, only to emerge and suddenly remember you forgot to ask a key question? A few moments of preparation can eliminate that problem.

An important motivational technique already discussed is speaking and writing clearly. Clarity is NOT overrated. Prep time gives you the opportunity to crystallize your thoughts and figure out the best, most succinct and powerful way to communicate them. Quality, well thought out communication is an art form and does not avail itself to those who fail to prepare.

ALL THINGS ARE READY, IF OUR MINDS BE SO
By Maria Stevens

As Shakespeare said, I believe the first key strategy of leadership framework is **Preparation**. Whether you are preparing to start the day, start the week, or engage in a 1:2:1 coaching session with a team member, you must prepare your approach. Remember, *every* interaction counts and your communication sends messages about your mood, your style and your receptivity to new ideas. From these interactions your team members are deciding how they will, in turn interact with you and your customers. As the leader you are setting the pace and in effect shaping the culture of your workplace. So, failure to adequately prepare for the day ahead can be destructive.

Years ago I had a leader who I'll refer to as Mark. Mark was an expert when it came to preparing for each and every team meeting and interaction. He taught me first-hand the value of being prepared with the right mindset and approach.

On many occasions my fellow sales reps and I would be engaged in fruitless conversations about sales minutia. Hours of conversation yielded few results.

In walks Mark. He would sit down and take in the conversation for a few minutes. Inevitably, he'd break in and ask us to "take a step back" from all of the current customer issues that we had been discussing and focus on our overall goal: helping our customers succeed. Mark was able to help us get back to basics and showed us that we were overcomplicating the basic principles of sales.

Mark seemed to have a way of drawing our best ideas out of us. Years later, Mark shared his strategy with me and it's the same one I'm sharing with you here.

Mark's approach was simply that he would *prepare* for these group and 1:1 interactions. When we were frustrated and experiencing a lack of creativity, Mark knew that his role in these sessions was to get us to think differently in order to *lead* us in the right direction. So instead of rushing into our account planning session after back-to-back calls, Mark closed his laptop, ignored his email and prepared for the session. He reviewed not only the objectives for the account planning session but he also spent time reminding himself of his goals as a leader. This ensured that when Mark joined our meeting, he engaged in a way that was consistent with his leadership principles.

This was Mark's leadership distinction that I grew to admire. When Mark participated in a meeting, you could always count on a productive conversation. He lead by example and demonstrated how engaging with a grounded approach yielded better outcomes. When Mark and I discussed his leadership philosophy during our many coaching sessions together, he emphasized the importance of being prepared and approaching every single activity and interaction with careful thought to the overall goals.

Mark also shared with me that regardless of what was on his schedule, he spent time reviewing his leadership goals on a daily basis. Over time, his "pre-game planning" of integrating his approach with his goals became like second nature.

Preparing your leadership approach is an excellent step toward creating a successful winning culture. Remember, it's about making the most out of each and every interaction and keeping your team members focused on what is truly important.

So don't 'wing-it' for your next coaching session with a rep. If you don't have enough time to prepare and regroup, reschedule the meeting. *Effective leaders don't manage in the moment. They carefully execute a well-thought out strategy for engaging, motivating and leading every single day.*

Maria Stevens specializes in coaching small business owners and sales professionals toward creating high-performing, profitable businesses. Maria is an expert resource for those looking for comprehensive strategies to create market differentiation and explosive sales results.

"**Luck is the residue of design.**"
                              Branch Rickey

Not convinced yet? Not sold on the idea that an ounce of prevention is worth a pound of cure? Does time spent in preparation still feel like wasted moments in this ready-shoot-aim world?

Branch Rickey was a Major League baseball player, General Manager and owner. He managed operations for multiple teams including the Brooklyn Dodgers in the 1940's.

Rickey essentially redesigned the minor league baseball system into what we know it as today: a training ground for the Major Leagues. It took him years to do that as he managed the St. Louis Cardinals but the results he gained were nothing less than astounding. His team became a dynasty winning several Pennants and World Series in the 1930's. Those successes were built on Rickey's concept of preparation.

Have you ever heard of some business owner who became an 'overnight success'? Did you think about how lucky that man or woman was? Must have been in the right place at the right time, you're thinking. Odds are good that if you did your research, you would find that he had worked hard for many years so that he would be in that right place. Or as Louis Pasteur said, *"Chance favors the prepared mind."*

Winning the lottery is luck. Hitting all 7's on the slot machine is luck. Building a business and taking advantage at the key moment in time is the residue of design. Training your mind to perceive opportunity where others only see problems is a trait the Roman philosopher, Seneca described well when he said, *"Luck is what happens when preparation meets opportunity."*

"For me the greatest beauty always lies in the greatest clarity."
                                    Gotthold Ephraim Lessing

      As Lessing suggests, strive to be a bit of a minimalist in communication. As you hire people and build your team, do your utmost to communicate clearly so that everyone will truly be on the same page.

      Again, this requires preparation. You do not want to expend massive efforts to hire the right people, put them in the right seats and then fail to communicate clearly with them.

      Strive for clarity in all your communications. Lessing called it 'the greatest beauty'. Not because of its artistic value but because of its rarity. Being able to communicate with your chosen team in a clear and succinct fashion is what will separate you from the din. Your voice needs to be heard above the fray not lost in the cacophonous drivel of daily visual and verbal transmissions. And you can achieve that when your message is clear.

      Shakespeare said, *"Brevity is the soul of wit."* In all your communication, rely on the popular business bromide: Be brief, be brilliant, be gone.

"If you don't know where you are going, you might wind up someplace else."

Yogi Berra

Ultimately, your duty as a manager is to lead. As Yogi so profoundly expressed, you truly need to know where you and your company are going so that you can clearly explain that to others.

Again, clarity is important here and while it is true that you do not have to be the source of all motivation, it is definitely your job to lead. You must be able to excite, inspire and energize your employees around the concept of where you are going. What do you hope to achieve? What is it that makes people want to come to work in the morning? It can be the pay, the camaraderie, the joy of the journey but, in the end, it also has to be the mission. And it is your job to identify that.

In today's world, most companies have Mission Statements precisely for this purpose. But that is the written word. You need to be able to verbalize that in voice and in actions so that your employees are all on board.

In the case of large high-profile companies it sometimes seems easier to state a bold exciting goal. Google's mission is *to organize the world's information and make it universally accessible and useful.* Wow! That is a dynamic goal and one that people can believe in on a philosophical level. So what is your goal if you are a dry cleaners in Casper, Wyoming? First of all, you are not in competition with Google on the world stage so just be yourself. Striving to be the best dry cleaners in town is an honorable and worthy goal that your employees can relate to. And when you have communicated that clearly to them, you will see that they take up that goal unto themselves. If you do well, you will be able to exclaim, as Robespierre said in 1789, "*I must see which way the crowd is headed, for I am their leader.*"

THE MIRACLE OF MAGGIE
As told by Betsy Dee

I needed a great personal assistant and I needed one yesterday. Yet another assistant had run screaming from the building when I looked in the mirror and said, *"Okay, so it's not them. It's you. Change it up."*

Easier said than done: After some deep soul searching, I identified what I call the Big Three:

1. I consistently endowed people with qualifications they never claimed to have. This was especially difficult to manage when they couldn't do the jobs I'd hired them for, because they didn't know how.

2. I steadfastly ignored my alarm sensors (so of course it always came as a shock when they went off). In one case, it took $15,000 worth of stolen merchandise for me to acknowledge that I'd overridden the weird vibes from the young lady I'd hired the month before.

3. I was so focused on filling an immediate (emergency) need I never asked myself, *"What's the net effect this candidate will have on my company?"* Little did I know that one such hire would cost me an IRS audit.

I was becoming the poster child for "What Never to Do In Business, Ever." when I finally zeroed in on the easily fixable mistake: *Forget "experience." Focus on "matching."*

I stumbled on this because I was so tired of being disappointed, annoyed, violated and homicidal I had finally become the skeptic I should have been all along. I interviewed three incredibly qualified candidates. On paper, they all had critical skills. So now the challenge was:

- Match their personality, energy level and work ethic to mine. I'm all about determination, resourcefulness, hard work, fearlessness and respect.
- Talk about their values. If they were at least similar to mine, we'd be able to work together through anything. I value true intelligence, but never at the expense of social grace. And I believe that Honesty + Diplomacy = Better Client Service.

- Match their broader skill set to what my job required: Client handling skills, Technology acumen, problem solving, detail management, self motivation and the flexibility to roll with punches!

And that is precisely how I found Maggie, my amazing, wow-tastic assistant of 18 months (and counting). It's also how I've filled positions as diverse as Art Director, Copywriter, Social Media Strategist, Web, Email and Flash Developer and Video Producer. And if I could offer any meaningful advice in the interview process, it's this:

- Build your list of Must-Haves before you even look for candidates.
- Listen very carefully. Take copious notes.
- NEVER hire until you've interviewed at least 3 others. Even if you think you have a winner.
- Instead of proposing the metrics of a Test Period, ask your candidate what they would propose. Their answer will offer a whole bunch of clues as to what their true objectives are.

In closing: Now, if I'm feeling *anything* beside "total confidence" in my candidate pool, I don't hire anyone. Hiring the wrong folks will cost me a lot more in the long run. Being more flexible in my definition of the right person saves me a lot of time, money and angst *today*.

Betsy Dee is the Owner, Creative Director and Chief Janitor of **betsy dee & co** in Oakland. As she says, "For most of my life, I've had my own business: In the theatre, fashion design and manufacturing, retail and advertising industries. This doesn't make me successful; it just makes me unemployable."
[Author's note: And clearly one smart cookie]

SUMMARY:

Building your team of employees and assigning the proper roles is the foundation of creating a dynamic and successful organization. Remember, that having the right people working for you is more important than having the right vision. In fact, many times the vision is merely a product of those right people and your course is literally determined for you by the company you keep.

Always:

- Go to great lengths to hire the right people. Cast a wide net and seek those who stand out. Set your standards high and expect integrity.
- Make sure everyone is in the right place. Find them the correct seat on the bus. Having a brilliant employee and putting her in the wrong role is like having no one at all. Match skills with roles but watch for those with a strong projected arc.
- Embrace preparation as a part of your arsenal. Use your time wisely to maximize the impact you have at meetings, in your writings and in your speech. Strive for the clarity that elevates your message above the daily business noise.
- Fine tune your mission statement so that you can express it in a way that clearly communicates how it relates to the everyday job. It IS your duty to explain it to the fine workers you have assembled. Failure to inspire and energize your people around the company goal will negate all your good work in the hiring arena.

When your organization is up and running with all the finest folks in the appropriate positions, you are ready to tackle all the other steps to building a spirited and motivated establishment. With the right people in the right spots, you are ready to excel at Greeting and Training.

CHAPTER FOUR

EXCEL AT "GREET AND TRAIN"

"A guest never forgets the host who had treated him kindly."
                                          Homer

    Imagine your last nervous steps as you walk towards the front door of the next company you are visiting to apply for a job. Then imagine that instead of a grumpy response from the receptionist when you ask for an application, you get a pleasant smile and a warm greeting. How's that for a start?

    Creating the right atmosphere for attracting high quality applicants begins at the front door. If applicants are treated kindly with a degree of common respect, your corporate image grows immensely. Perhaps they are seated in a conference room, offered a cup of coffee and a take-home brochure designed specifically for applicants. Maybe a video could be played describing what the company does, what it stands for and what opportunities are available.

    Would you want to work at such a place? Who wouldn't? It's a cliché now but 'You never get a second chance to make a first impression' is true not just for the applicant but also for the company. There may not be a job for that applicant but she will speak highly of you nonetheless. And if there is a job, the new hire will begin with nothing but favorable thoughts about their new venture.

    Be the host by whom you would want to be received.

NOBODY EVER TOLD ME THAT ...

Alisa timidly knocked on my open office door and peered in. I looked up from my desk and waved her towards me. I knew it was her first day as a Customer Service Rep and I had been expecting her.

We exchanged some small talk about how she had come to interview and be hired and then I got down to my real purpose. I felt that I needed to reach the new hires on a different level so I tried something I had never done before.

For about ten minutes I talked to Alisa about "The Big Picture". I did something that no employer I ever worked for had ever done with me. I talked UP to Alisa and told her all about what we are "really" doing.

Talking about the big picture is a calm, mature and hopefully inspiring conversation about your industry. In my case, I was talking about my courier business. So I would take a few moments to describe how the industry began; how as time became more important, the need for faster delivery generated higher demand. Then I would talk about our customers and what they do and how we help them. Finally, I would elaborate on the impact we have and how completing a delivery on time might assist our client in landing a big account or expanding faster and generating new jobs. I'd go on for quite a while talking about how our company fit into the overall economy and how we helped our customers in some small way to achieve their dreams.

Then, I brought it all back to Alisa and her job. I told her how she would have an impact; how she personally could help others to make their goals and perhaps to assist in the creation of jobs for others. I explained how important it was for her to take the orders swiftly and accurately with a maximum of courtesy to the caller. I really wanted to give some deeper meaning to each specific act within her job description and I was hoping that this new approach might do just that.

All the while, Alisa sat demurely, listening courteously and patiently hearing me out. She had probably heard some variation of this in the interview but not from me and not in this kind of detail. When I finished, she looked at me a bit wide-eyed and I feared I had missed the mark.

She added to my fears with one short sentence. She looked at me sincerely and said, *"No one ever told me anything like that before..."*

And then she set my fears aside as this young new hire smiled and said, *"...and it was wonderful! I've never worked anywhere where I was explained what the company is really doing and how I fit in. It means a lot to me that you told me that. And I understand why Linda was training me so hard today on some of the details. We've all got a big responsibility here."*

Our meeting ended and as she left the room I breathed a huge sigh of relief. My description of the big picture DID seem to hit a chord with her and help her understand and value the aspects of her job that would impact others. Later, I found that talking UP to my employees and sharing more views of the big picture were some of the best conversations I ever had. I learned to appreciate and value those moments that this simple tactic produced and, as usual, to kick myself for not learning this lesson faster.

GB

"In order to properly understand the big picture, everyone should fear becoming mentally clouded and obsessed with one small section of the truth."

Xun Zi

People's work product is more likely to be superior when they fully understand the big picture. A worker on an assembly line performing the same act over and over again may feel that his whole world is focused on one singular function. After a time, that function may seem small and meaningless. It would be easy to imagine apathy and inattentiveness resulting.

That is where you, the manager, come in. If the worker understands the 'big picture', attitudes can change. Perhaps the assembly line example is extreme but every employee in any position, particularly front line and entry level personnel tend to be focused on a few basic tasks. Your job is to make sure they understand how they fit into the overall scheme of the company.

Take time during the training process to explain how their actions intertwine with everyone else's. Illustrate what happens when they do their job correctly ... and what occurs when they don't. Paint a picture of the end user of your product or service and describe their reaction when all has been done well ... and when it hasn't. Tie your employee into a piece of the responsibility for their actions and help them extract some of the same pleasure you do when the business meets its duty to the customer.

"The training of children is a profession where we must know how to waste time in order to save it."
Jean-Jacques Rousseau

Our employees are not our children but the principal is the same. Often, training seems to be this big necessary evil that gets in the way of real work. When you need 'a body' right away to fill a gap, training simply slows down progress. So, we fail to do it properly.

The first way to avoid this issue is to plan and prepare properly. Anticipating the need for new hires can minimize manpower surprises. Is it always just bad luck that put you into a manpower shortage situation? If luck is the residue of design then bad luck must be the residue of poor design.

Having a well prepared training program in place with reading materials and videos is a step in the right time-saving direction. Hiring before the need is another. But, ultimately, failing to take the time to train new hires properly will cost you more in the long run. Poorly trained workers create problems that are far more expensive than the brief training time required to do it right.

Rousseau recognized that training is perceived as a waste of time but the disciplined manager knows it must be done anyway. And that manager knows it is not truly wasted. It is an investment in the employee that will pay small but frequent dividends down the road.

> "After base pay, career advancement and training tend to be the most valued elements of the employment deal for young workers."
>
> Mercer's *What's Working* Survey

In October of 2011, Mercer published its "What's Working™" Survey. From Q4 2010 to Q2 2011, they surveyed over 30,000 employees in 17 world markets to gain new insights into the minds of today's workforce. The results were intriguing. The analysis identified <u>two</u> particularly compelling insights about the youngest workers in the workforce.

The first of these was that younger Generation Y and Millennials are far more likely to be satisfied in their jobs and yet still inclined to seek other opportunities. In response to the statement, "At the present time, I am seriously considering leaving my organization," scores for the youngest workers (ages 16 to 24) were 10 percentage points higher than the 25-34 age group.

This creates a unique dilemma for today's employers. With the younger workers, there is no strong sense of allegiance to the company nor is there an expectation of long-term employment. Even when the worker is generally satisfied with the organization they work for, they are still more inclined to consider moving on.

In light of this apparent lack of loyalty, what can the employer do to counteract the negative effects of losing key young workers? Mercer's study also identified what most motivates younger employees. In order, Base Pay, Career Advancement, Training, Type of Work, Bonus/Incentives and Flexible Work Schedules. As Mercer states, "... with many career-related (employer) scores remaining below the 50% mark, ... many companies are implicitly saying to at least half of their employees, 'Satisfy your career desires by leaving'.

Meanwhile, those companies that are making a concerted effort to respond to young workers' career needs are hooking the best talent, fueling their talent pipeline and gaining a competitive advantage.

The second insight into the mind of young workers is that younger workers today have more in common across all borders than do older colleagues. That is, today's young people think far more alike, regardless of nationality, than older workers do. Cultural norms are being bended as we speak.

One of the main reasons for this is the advancements in technology. This younger generation is a tech-savvy, app-oriented group that multitasks with ease and expects something different out of the work experience. They are more interested in a collaborative workplace, scheduling flexibility, frequent interaction and feedback and, as Mercer states "fairly immediate gratification for their efforts."

As Mercer points out, "But it's important to remember that Millennials aren't the only generation taking advantage of social media tools and new technology. Whether you are an employee seeking a career move or an employer seeking the next great hire, social media participation is essential. HR processes and communication must adapt to reflect these changes."

Companies today must adapt and find ways to capitalize on these insights. As the older workforce rotates out, the challenge for employers will be to maintain an active talent pipeline that gives the younger workers the motivation to stay and advance in their careers with that same organization.

And finally, in light of the similarities between young people worldwide, multinational organizations have a unique opportunity to gain huge economies of scale if they can restructure and operate more consistently across borders.

To view more detail on the results of the Mercer's What's Working™ Survey, visit www.mercer.com.

"It does not matter how slowly you go so long as you do not stop."

> Confucius

Our first logical reaction to this saying by Confucius is to set it aside; to disregard it as old school thinking; to discount its relevance in our 'I-need-it-yesterday' world.

That would be a mistake. Steeped in Chinese tradition, is the long term outlook adopted in much of what they do. Confucius is not talking about moving slowly in a single deed. Rather he is speaking to our larger endeavors as in building a business. This thought brings us back to commitment and the value of a steadfast course of action.

Too many times, companies have adopted a philosophy of operating but have failed to embrace the commitment to that philosophy which must go along with it. The pace of change has sped up dramatically but gaining the fruits of Corporate Change is not an overnight process. It requires long range thinking and an earnest and eager assumption of the philosophy behind it.

Training is, as we know, viewed as an unproductive and inconvenient interruption to the actual business cycle. It seems to move slowly and the results are not always immediately evident. But it is a key component to building a future and becoming the kind of company in which all employees are on the same page.

To create a company full of motivated, inspired, engaged employees, you must first make the decision to begin your long journey with a single step. And then, armed with your faith, do not stop.

THE PERFECT TRAINER

I had run my courier service company in Seattle for 25 years before I discovered a key error in my ways. When a new courier would come to work for us, he or she was usually experienced in most aspects of doing an actual physical delivery. However, we still needed to train them on our paperwork, our "radio protocol" (which we called it even after we stopped using radios and switched to cell phones) and other unique dispatch practices that we utilized. Just to make it more difficult, we operated quite differently from other courier services so it was a challenge to bring new folks up to speed quickly.

Naturally, when I was searching around for someone to assign to the task of training the new drivers, I would consistently pick one of our existing drivers who had shown impressive skills on the road. I wanted the very best driver I had training people and showing them the ropes. Makes sense, right?

If you look at your own company, I'll bet you would do the same. You don't want a poor performer to train new people. And you wouldn't want anyone who did not display good work habits and high productivity, right? Of course not, so you probably have your best workers train the new hires. Makes all the sense in the world ...

...except it doesn't. And it took me more than two decades to figure that out. Hey, I'm a consistent plodder, not a genius.

It happened at a meeting with my Operations Management team. We were bemoaning the latest set of problems created by new drivers who did not follow proper procedures. *"Why O why,"* I cried, *"are these new guys so clueless? We trained them on this. They are supposed to know it. What happened to the good old days when guys like Rick and Chuck and Phil were coming on board and became superstars overnight?"*

Turns out my memory was a bit foggy. No one was a superstar overnight but as the company got larger and technology invaded our world, the job had gotten more complex. There were more details to remember and less margin for error. Mistakes we made "in the old days" were not caught and reported by the watchful eye of the computer.

Still, we trained them, why weren't they getting it? After bouncing that question around a bit, I found out that the new drivers were not remembering all the details because there were so many ... and because our trainers were delivering them in the same way they delivered packages ... with all due haste! The trainers were telling them everything but they weren't communicating. They were glossing over details and doing what had always worked well for them before ... working quickly.

Enter Dave. Dave was a very competent courier for us but he was older, more experienced in life, and a calm easy going fellow. We asked Dave to do some training because we thought he might slow down the conversation pace a bit and make more headway with the new drivers.

The results were staggering. Many new drivers reported that they had a "pleasant training session" with Dave and understood what had to be done now. Dave slowed down the communication and made sure his trainee understood each point before moving on to the next one. He asked a lot of questions like *"Does that make sense to you?"* and *"Am I going too fast?"* Dave had finely tuned listening skills so he waited to get the feedback he needed before moving on. We saw positive results immediately!

Yes, it was a simple lesson but it was learned the hard way. When selecting a trainer, make sure they are a <u>communicator</u> **first** and a star performer **second**.

GB

"Excellence is an art won by training and habituation. We do not act rightly because we have virtue or excellence, but we rather have those because we have acted rightly. We are what we repeatedly do. Excellence, then, is not an act but a habit."

Aristotle

Getting your tennis serve delivered into that perfect spot; firing arrows into the bulls eye at the archery range; making the soccer ball bend as it flies into the goal. These are wondrous acts that happen because the athlete practiced and trained repeatedly over and over again. No one who understands sports believes otherwise. And yet, in business, we often expect excellence to occur with little or no training.

Aristotle was not someone most of us would care to debate. He certainly had an insightful mind and here he reminds us that good acts are often the effect of good training. That repeatedly showing an employee the correct way to handle a problem can produce the positive results we are after.

Yet, most businesses choose to debate Aristotle. They say, *"We just want to expect our people to do it right the first time. We told them how and if they can't do it right, we'll find someone who can."*

Perhaps the fault is not theirs. Possibly it is your training process that is faulty or your follow-up/follow through that is suspect. Workers will do the 'virtuous' act when they have been trained effectively to do it. Excellence is a habit. It is your job to cultivate it.

> **"Experience is a hard teacher because she gives the test first, the lesson afterwards."**
>
> Vernon Sanders Law

There is another saying that goes "The only training for leadership is leadership." Yes, we have all been there. Experience IS a hard teacher. As managers, you are essentially learning on the job daily. The number of times you must do something you have never done before increases as you rise up the ladder. You are faced with trying to draw on the experience of similar past events and somehow divine your way through the latest crisis.

And, yes, all the lessons come after the fact. So how do you navigate through that and avoid failure? Well, you don't. Failure is inevitable at some point or another so come to grips with that. Remember the old bromide: If you are not failing, you are not trying hard enough. The goal is not to avoid failure but to succeed in such a way that you minimize the effects of failure. Failure in itself is not a bad thing. When Thomas Edison was criticized for failing to invent the electric light bulb after thousands of attempts, he exclaimed, *"I have not failed 1,000 times. I have successfully discovered 1,000 ways to NOT make a light bulb!"*

Small failures are the price you pay for your management education. What you learn from those is far more valuable than any knowledge from a string of successes. With success you learn what happened to work that one time. With failure you learned what doesn't work and you know not to go down that road again.

How you handle a defeat is just as important. In trying to build a company full of motivated, empowered employees, you have a great opportunity to set an example. Be open about your failure. Discuss it with your employees. Dissect it. Analyze why it did not work and share that so others may learn too. Help your employees to realize that failure is not to be feared but the willingness to confront it is.

"Feelings of worth can flourish only in an atmosphere where individual differences are appreciated, mistakes are tolerated, communication is open, and rules are flexible - the kind of atmosphere that is found in a nurturing family."

                                              Virginia Satir

Ms. Satir, an author and psychotherapist, should have been a business consultant too. Here she talks about personal feelings of self-worth but what she refers to could easily be applied to the atmosphere in business surroundings.

Part of greeting and training properly is introducing your new hires to your company and helping them acclimate. As you do that on their first day, they will get a lasting impression of the kind of company they are joining. That business ambiance is the one you, as manager, have created. Whatever it is that the new hire sees, is what they will come to understand as the norm.

Have you ever visited a school and found the staff and teachers to be serious, quiet and not particularly warm. And then you meet the Principal and find that the workers are truly emulating their leader. Or perhaps you have made a call on a small company where you are greeted warmly and everyone you meet has a smile and is laughing or seemingly enjoying their work. Odds are that the owner or manager is of the same ilk.

Once again, it is apparent that as manager, this really IS all about you. Your attitude is contagious and flows downhill. A hard driving manager who has no time for small talk or joviality, will create an atmosphere where mistakes are not tolerated, communication is closed, humor is absent and fear is the primary motivator. And in that non-nurturing atmosphere, open discourse is a rarity, new ideas die a lonely death and finding joy in the work is beyond unlikely.

Don't be that manager. Be the other guy.

SUMMARY:

Pay now or pay later. That is your mantra concerning training. Training isn't limited to just showing a new hire how to do their specific job. It is also training your new team member how to interact and participate with the other employees. It is training him or her about your corporate culture and how you expect excellence, trust and sincere effort.

- Start applicants out right. Show your best side and make your company a highly desirable place to work.
- Share the big picture. Make sure every new hire understands what role they play and how their work affects everyone else.
- Find a way to make time for quality training. Create an effective training program that can, if necessary, be launched on short notice. Discipline yourself to make the time for proper training available.
- Keep in mind the changing demographic forces that are at play today. Younger employees are more likely to move on unless you give them good reasons to stay. Your investment in training cannot pay off if they leave.
- Make sure your trainers are first rate communicators.
- Remember that the cost of ineffective training is never evident up front. It is a bill that comes payable much later and always cost more than the initial training would have.

So now you have a company with dynamic employees, all in the right roles, in a positive frame of mind and well trained. Your next step is to insure that each and every one of them is motivated by the opportunity to affect the size of their own paycheck: Incentivize, Bonus and Reward.

CHAPTER FIVE

INCENTIVIZE, BONUS AND REWARD

"If winning isn't everything, why do they keep score?"
                                       Vince Lombardi

Possibly one of the most repeated sports quotes of all time is this statement from the great Vince Lombardi.

Yes, in America, we keep score. Getting a monthly Profit and Loss Statement is a bit like getting a report card in school. It is partly a game and partly an up-to-date assessment of your personal management skills. And every manager or business owner should look at that P&L as a referendum on their management decisions and style.

To a somewhat lesser degree, your employees are keeping score too. Their paychecks are their report cards. In the case of commissioned sales people, that is far too true. For the rank and file hourly employees it is a slow moving truth that rarely changes.

Think about that. Do your employees feel good about their report card? Is there anything more you can do to make them feel like it is an equitable trade: their time for your money?

Winning would make it more than equitable. And workers win when they feel appreciated, respected, involved, motivated and empowered. And if you can help them to feel that way AND make the daily work part of a fun and exciting journey, then you are winning too.

OPENING THE BOOKS AND PLAYING GAMES
FOR FUN AND PROFIT
By Jack Stack

The Book Source Inc. a $31-million distributor of educational trade books, is on a mission to provide teachers across the country with appropriate paperback books children will actually read. At the close of 2004, the St. Louis based company was tracking to do $20 million in sales through its retail division alone, but due to the loss of a large contract, the owners decided to abandon the retail market and focus exclusively on the wholesale market.

By 2007, the company's plan to make this enormous change was in full swing. The COO and co-owner, Gary Jaffe used the concepts explained in my book, *"The Great Game of Business"* to engage and motivate his 65 employees, particularly those in the company's two bindery locations. *"Our critical number is the number of hours it takes to produce 'x' number of books."* Jaffe explained. *"We call it books per person hours, or BPH."* In keeping with the Great Game of Business principles, all employees participated in monthly companywide financial meetings and weekly department huddles. Everyone at every level were given the tools and authority to implement business-process and cultural changes that would enhance the new, open environment. They also developed more family-friendly policies and benefits such as a wellness program, flextime and 'bring your baby to work.'

As a result of exposing the employees to a greater understanding of the company's financial numbers and to efforts to include everyone in the participation of the 'game', results came quickly. Within a year, their Steelville bindery team improved its BPH from 6 to 9, for a 50% increase in productivity. The team at the Farmington location moved its BPH from 15 to 20, for a 33% gain. Jaffe reports that better systems and training led to a steep reduction in the number of hours worked. *"Our overtime hours in 2006 were 25,500; in 2007 they were about*

3,300." Jaffe said. *"This improvement alone produced a savings of almost $311,000."*

COO Jaffe attributes 100% of Booksource's success to his employees. By challenging the employees and turning work into more of a game, they learned volumes about the business, but more importantly, they learned how profitable it can be to trust, respect and help one another. The new motivational bonus plan, the regular huddles, the friendly competition and the flexible production schedule all worked together to encourage employees to think and act more like owners. In 2007, the team achieved <u>perfect</u> attendance and substantially higher levels of productivity in fewer hours.

Meantime, the strategic shift away from retail sales has paid off. Since 2004, Booksource's educational division has experienced annual double digit–plus growth. As President Neil Jaffe said, "Even with the lower total dollar sales, our profitability is higher and more consistent than it was prior to our exit from sales to retailers."

This is just one example of many companies who have unleashed the power of Open-Book Management. When you can engage and involve your employees and empower them to achieve their goals, bottom line results can improve dramatically.

Jack Stack is the founder and CEO of SRC Holdings, a company comprising more than 35 separate companies. SRC's companies do everything from consulting to packaging to building high-performance engines. He is the author of *"The Great Game of Business"* and has been dubbed "The Father of Open-Book Management."

> "So here we are: in the country that founded the free enterprise system, facing the greatest economic crisis of our lifetimes, and we are doing battle against those forces armed with the strategy of paying people for showing up."
>
> Gary Brose

Yes, that is what we do. We hire people and we agree to pay them a salary in return for their promise to show up and try. And, yes, there are minimum wage laws in this country that we all have to abide by but nowhere does it say that everything we pay them must be paid in return for showing up. There is another way.

Consider the concept of decreasing starting pay by, say, 10% and adding a performance bonus equal to that same 10%. Design the performance bonus so that when the new hire performs to the degree expected, she gets it. And if she doesn't, she doesn't. And if she exceeds it, she gets something more.

Quit paying people just for showing up. Reward them on payday for actually performing. If you examine any job in your business, you should be able to identify one or two actions that each employee takes which affect the bottom line. Use the one that can be objectively counted and set a goal for that employee. Be creative. Warehouse Manager: less than X% damaged goods; Receptionist: zero customer complaints about phone etiquette; Delivery Driver: Y% on-time deliveries; Phone Order Takers: Over Z% of phone calls answered before the second ring.

If you demand nothing, that is what you may get. But if you insist on a bare minimum standard and entice with the possibility of making more if that standard is exceeded, you will begin to reach new levels of motivation. Pay for performance, not promises.

THE EIGHT ESSENTIAL ELEMENTS

When I bought my first business, a small messenger service in Seattle, I was convinced that motivating the couriers to be productive was the key to long term success. So I embarked on what would turn out to be a 25 year quest to design the perfect bonus program. OK, if anyone had told me that it was going to take me 25 years (or even 5 or 10), I doubt that I would have continued. But my conviction was strong and my head was hard and I just muddled my way through those decades thinking I was ever so close to the answer.

Well, I slowly learned what worked and what didn't. I identified hundreds of methods that did not work. I think I invented half of them myself! I treated my company like my own private Petri dish, experimenting repeatedly with all sorts of off-the-wall ideas. Eventually, I discovered certain principles that seemed to hold true for every successful plan I put into place.

Now bear in mind, I did this all in the real world; in real time; with real people. This wasn't theoretical. Some of the feedback I got came in the form of curses and tears. Some came via anonymous hate mail. Much more came in strained diplomatic phrases as employees struggled to educate me and tell me what was wrong with my latest game plan.

In 2006, it dawned on me that I had spent most of my business life in pursuit of a dream ... to find the perfect bonus program that would act as a constant motivator for everyone in the company. And in the process, I found I had identified the Eight Essential Elements of a Successful Bonus Program. I found it hard to believe that anyone else had ever been so stubborn and pig-headed to spend that much time in pursuit of Bonus Nirvana so I decided I better share what I had learned. By 2008, I finished my first book, _"Bonus Your Way to Profits"._

THE EIGHT ESSENTIAL ELEMENTS OF A QUALITY BONUS PROGRAM

Listed below is a very short summary of the Eight Essential Elements of a Successful Bonus Program:

GRADIATED - Tier your bonuses. Structure the bonuses so that there are 3 to 5 levels. Make the first easy to reach for someone who is doing the job reasonably well. The middle tier bonus is a reward for doing "quite well" while the last level(s) are for record-breaking performance. Creating multiple levels gives your employees one more goal to shoot for and several opportunities for celebrating as they reach each tier.

EQUITABLE - The bonus amount must be fair and equitable. If you have many people in the company on various bonus programs, one program cannot be so good that everyone else wants to change jobs to get to it. Making one bonus program too lucrative in comparison to others will foster ill will between departments and damage morale.

TIMELY - The frequency of the bonus should vary inversely with the level of the employee. Lower level or entry employees should get paid their bonus frequently as in once every payday or once every month. Middle level Managers should be paid monthly for the previous month's performance or at the least, Quarterly. Senior Management can be rewarded once per year. The key is to make the reward payment happen often enough that the thought of it affects daily duties. When you can drill down to the individual act that is measured by the bonus program, you are providing true motivation for good performance. This is extremely important. If you do everything else correctly but fail to pay in a timely manner, the entire bonus program will fail.

SIMPLE - Keep it simple: Simple to understand; simple to calculate and simple to explain. Clearly explain how your bonus program works in writing and make the computation of it so simple that anyone can understand it or do the math themselves. In many cases, it is even more effective if you let the employees compute results themselves. If they don't understand it, they won't be able to explain it to anyone else and they ultimately won't care.

MEANINGFUL - The bonus must be meaningful on two levels. First, it must be based on an action that is relevant to the employee's job function. In other words, the employees have to be able to affect results. Second, it must be a large enough amount of money to be meaningful to the employee. A good rule of thumb is to structure the bonus to pay, on the middle tier, about 6 to 8% of the employee's base pay for the relevant time period. If the middle tier pays out less than 6% of the pay period's base pay, it is too low to motivate. If it pays higher than 8%, it is overkill. Save the higher percentages for the level or levels above the middle.

OBJECTIVE -The bonus must be based on objective rather than subjective points. Base the bonus on something that can be counted without ambiguity. For example, base the bonus on the number of widgets sold each pay period or month. Or the number of consecutive days when Quality Control shows a 95% service level. Do not base it on how management perceives the employee is performing or on how well employees dress for work. Nothing should be subjective. Subjective goals are subject to personal biases and always engender mistrust of management. Always base your bonus program on things you can count.

REINFORCED - Feedback, feedback, feedback. Give the employees a daily or frequent periodic recap of their performance as it relates to the bonus. Post the results for all to see if it is appropriate. Team goal bonuses should always be posted on the wall and updated daily. Make sure everyone knows how they are doing and how likely it is that they will hit bonus level 1, 2, or 3 (or 4 or 5). Remember that every time you remind employees about their progress toward their goal, you are reinforcing its importance and mentally tying the reward to the act. You cannot do that too often!

EASY- Yes, we already discussed making it easy to understand, but also make it somewhat easy to succeed. Bonuses work best in an environment where base pay is artificially lower than the norm but the bonuses are consistent and attainable. Set the first tier bonus at a level that an average performance can achieve so that nearly everyone gets "something". Set the next higher levels to be more challenging and skewer them up so that the greater the achievement the greater the reward….in a big way!

Create your bonus program correctly and the employee, the company and everyone
GETS MORE!

Visit www.SmallBizSherpa.com for more details.
Copyright 2006 Gary Brose.
All rights reserved.

"Call it what you will, incentives are what get people to work harder."

Nikita Khrushchev

If you did a double-take when you read this quote, you were not alone. The fact that the leader of the nation that founded Communism would openly admit such a thing is mindboggling. And yet, there it is in black and white: Nikita Khrushchev lauding one of the pillars of the free enterprise system.

This is like cats admiring dogs; Democrats praising Republicans; Red Sox flattering the Yankees. When an American industrialist sings the praises of capitalism it is considered routine. But when the head communist agrees that workers perform better when given incentives, it erases all doubts about the statement's veracity.

And yet, many companies continue to ignore proven methods of motivation in the workplace. Thousands of companies in America continue to pay people a base wage with no other incentives and no hope for significant rewards for excellent performance.

Each business owner or manager should ask themselves what they are doing to provide incentives for their workforce. Appreciating people, acknowledging success, praising, delegating and building a participatory atmosphere are all important steps but everyone keeps score by the size of their paycheck. If you are not financially rewarding high levels of performance you are failing to put your money where your mouth is. Recognize all-star behavior with raises, bonuses, awards and programs that systematically motivate through the pocketbook.

Don't be like Nikita. All talk, no action.

TURNING YOUR BUSINESS AROUND WITH PAY FOR PERFORMANCE
By Robert Papes

I was once contracted to manage the business of a Fortune 500 company in Ohio. This company, which was going down the tube at warp speed, paid their top management 50% of their bonuses on the profit performance of the total business. While this is pretty standard stuff, they didn't define how it could be generated. The business was making products for their sister plants overseas. The division controller who also worked directly for this business and whose bonus was directly impacted by their profit results, arranged to transfer 50% of their sales to a sister plant at much higher than budgeted margins.

The business didn't find new external customers, didn't develop new business, charged the customer's of their sister plants higher prices than were budgeted and yet the management got paid obscene bonuses. I mean really obscene, since their budget didn't forecast their shipping products overseas at high margins. When I was brought in as a general manager to turn the business around, I was greeted by bad news. The overseas shipments stopped the month after I got there, 50% of their business went out the door without so much as a prospect in the pipeline. The management left the business in a situation where it would start losing money immediately. Yet, they had received obscene bonuses for 'beating their prior year income budget.'

I made sure that the bonuses being paid were for real results and not just accounting voodoo. For the sales folks, I changed the bonus program to reward prospecting and adding new accounts that generated true profit. The bottom line: three consecutive years of new business totaling 20+ percent of total sales in a stagnant industry. And a happy, motivated management team that made it all happen!

The lesson is to not only set goals, but to also always define how the goal must be achieved, that is, by their own individual efforts and not by a windfall. How goals and objectives are achieved is as important as achieving them.

The principal here is pretty straight forward, yet it is amazing how many businesses get it wrong. You must not only tie bonuses directly to the results you want, but you must also define how they must accomplish these results. Tie that in with a mutually agreed upon set of goals and a bonus plan that shares excess profit with those who make it happen and you have a true formula for any turn-around.

> Robert Papes has extensive experience turning businesses around. As a general manager, Bob has engineered five consecutive business turnarounds of monumental proportions. As a consultant, Bob has helped over seventy small businesses all over the country improve their bottom lines. In his book, <u>Management During an Economic Crisis</u>, he shares with the reader what works and the **why** and **how** of it all.

"Success is the ability to go from one failure to another with no loss of enthusiasm."
                                   Winston Churchill

Many managers will not embark on a new venture unless they have total confidence it will work. Sometimes it is hard to get to that point so inevitably there comes a point in time when the manager must pass on the project or stick his neck out and give it a shot.

A good way to move forward even when you are not necessarily confident of success is to gather your project participants and have a heart-to-heart chat about what you are about to do. In this meeting, it would be acceptable, even laudatory, for you to admit your concerns and openly say *"We're going to go forward with this even though it may fail."* And then follow that up with *"We will either succeed or we will learn enough to do it right the next time."*

Designing a new bonus program often goes through the same cycle. It is difficult to anticipate every objection, quirk or surprising side effect of experimenting with motivation. This author designed a bonus program for the call center operators designed to reward more efficient phone performance. The first six months required five tweaks and changes. It wasn't until the sixth iteration of the bonus plan that we got it right. But we told everyone that our goal was to structure the program so that it rewarded everyone fairly; provided proper motivation and feedback; and created the results that the company wanted in order to justify the cost. Each time we made a change, it was seen as a step toward perfecting the plan, rather than an admission of failure. With that attitude, everyone embraced change eagerly and the journey itself was much more enjoyable.

"A man who trusts nobody is apt to be the kind of man nobody trusts."

Harold MacMillan

One of the key elements in creating an effective bonus, incentive pay or rewards system is your credibility. Your employees must believe that you will be true to your word and honest in your dealings with them.

When you hear some business managers say sarcastic things like *"Oh, we're management. No one trusts us."* do you ever wonder if, perhaps, they are getting what they deserve? If the employee base does not trust you it is probably because you haven't given them any good reasons to do so. Do you always keep your word? Do you follow up as you said you would? Do you award bonus payments properly? Or do you find excuses not to pay?

Trust is an essential element to any incentive program you design. If you hesitate to reward as promised because suddenly cash flow is tight or because you calculated the bonus differently than the employee did, then you are destroying all future good faith efforts by the employees. No employee will go the extra mile if they feel they will be cheated out of their reward later.

The best bonus programs work when employees have full confidence that they will be treated fairly when they meet their goals. Always agree on the formula calculation in advance and then let the employee do the math themselves. When you repeatedly pay out incentive pay as promised, you build on your credibility and move yourself into a position to be able to demand more from people because they will trust you and believe in you. The dividends the company gets from that belief system far outweigh the costs. Be fair. Be truthful. Be consistent.

> "My goal in sailing isn't to be brilliant or flashy in individual races, just to be consistent over the long run."
>
> Dennis Conner

Sometimes the simplest thoughts are the most insightful. Dennis Conner, the four time winner of the Americas Cup in sailboat racing, set his goal to "just be consistent".

Just be consistent: Sounds mundane. Almost as if he is underachieving. And yet, being truly consistent is a rarity in both life and management.

In a business sense, it is an under-appreciated trait. But if you think back to your childhood, remember how confused you were when your mother or father would tell you to do something and then, later, say to do the opposite? Your employees look to you for guidance. When they see you discipline one employee for a transgression and look the other way for someone else, you are being inconsistent too. Striving to be consistent is far more important than it seems. And actually being consistent enhances your power, your strength and your credibility.

In motivating employees, inconsistency can defeat you as quickly as any error. Creating an incentive pay plan and paying it out properly does more than reward people financially. It propels them forward to want to try harder. When they fully believe that their efforts will be recognized, appreciated AND monetarily compensated, they will try harder to continue that success. But if you are unpredictable and adjust bonus amounts on the fly or equivocate and delay payments, employee attitudes will turn sour and employee confidence will wane. All future bonus program efforts will be tainted.

Be like Dennis. Set your goal to be consistent.

"Life is a game. Money is how we keep score."
                                    Ted Turner

Do you take yourself very seriously? Is there immense pressure on you to increase profits? Do you feel overwhelmed and burdened by the imperative to make money? Sounds like you forgot it was a game.

And it is. Granted, it is a serious game and much rides on the outcome. But it is life too. And you cannot live every day bearing the desperate anxiety of worrying about this month's numbers. To truly do well as a manager of people, you need to relax and enjoy the game. Everything in your organization flows from you. You set the tone. If you are wired and uptight, your employees will be the same. If you are calm and relaxed and focused on doing your best, your employees will emulate that as well.

It is a game. And it will be played no matter what. If it's going to be played anyway, you might as well try to enjoy it. Share the adventure of the great game of business with your employees. Get them involved. Let them share in the glory of a "well-played" day and feel a little of the pain of a setback. Success is sweeter when failure was possible. Winning is better when everyone saw defeat lurking around the corner.

It is a game. Play it. Take pleasure in the excitement of it, give it your best and let the cards fall where they may. The final score may not always be what you like. In fact, if you are a manager for long, it is a given that you will lose some and win some. Cultivate that same appreciation in your people and share the wins and losses together.

Money IS how we keep score. But long after the money is gone, the only thing you will remember is the game and the joy you gained in playing it.

MEET ME AT THE TUGBOAT

Returning now to Seattle entrepreneur John Scholl as he told me this story in his own words:

I wanted to do something special for my employees. We had had a decent year profit wise at BIGink, not a record breaker but a good year for a business our size. I wanted to reward the employees; I wanted to express my appreciation for their hard work; to give them a special and unique experience that they would value; and I wanted to make it a bit of a team-building event.

So after considering all the possibilities, I decided to do something I'd never seen done before. I gave everyone T-shirts with the company name, BIGink, in big bold letters printed on the front and back and I asked them all to wear them to a meeting. I picked a Saturday and told everyone to bring their spouses or significant others to a brunch at a nearby mall. I said, *"Let's all meet at the tugboat in the center of the mall at 10am and then from there we will go to brunch together."* OK, sounds a bit pedestrian but it was a free meal, right, so everyone showed up. That's when I surprised them. I gathered everyone around me and handed out envelopes with two $100 bills in them to each employee. Then I told them we were going to brunch at noon at a restaurant in the mall and that their job for the next two hours was to go out and spend as much of that $200 on anything they wanted to buy. But there was a catch: They had to spend it <u>ALL</u> or turn in the remainder to me!

They went nuts! I had all these employees and their families running around the mall in my company t-shirts buying things that they had denied themselves before. Ever gone shopping for essentials and seen that one item that you didn't need but really wanted? And so you pass it up and do the practical thing and suddenly shopping is just work and no fun. Well, today, they <u>had</u> to buy it and they

83

were required to bring their purchases to the brunch so we could all do a "show and tell". I told them I expected them to WOW each other with the surprising items they had bought.

They had a great time making their purchase decisions. They showed them off and laughed and turned our brunch into an incredible bonding event. I took a few moments and talked about each employee there, praising them individually for their efforts and made sure the family members or significant others saw just how special their loved one was ... to me and to their co-workers. This was exactly the kind of event I had hoped to create. Could I have just added $200 to their year-end checks? Sure, and what fun would that have been? By doing a "Mall Raid" and the brunch, they experienced a team-building event, a huge surprise, a venue for showing off to their family and a moment in time that I am confident they will remember and tell others about. Beats a $200 bonus on the check any day!

> John Scholl's company, BIGink, is a leading printer and graphic arts company in the Seattle area.

"Men are moved by two levers only: Fear and self interest."
                                    Napoleon Bonaparte

Sounds a bit crass. But if you think about it, you may agree that the Little General was on to something.

Fear and self interest: levers of motivation. Can you think of anything else that motivates people? Perhaps just good will or altruism. However, if you dig deeper, isn't every altruistic act done because the doer feels a deep need to do it. Isn't that self interest?

So, if the only two levers of motivation are fear and self interest, which one do you want to work with? You can try to build an organization based on fear and many before you have. Make those employees fearful for their jobs. Craft a fear of error or simply a fear of you. That would be one road to go down.

Another is to accept that workers are motivated by self interest and to find ways to make that work for you and the company. Employees today have an interest in many things: advancement, money, praise, recognition, titles and more. Find a way to make that work for you.

The best advice? Communicate clearly with your people and make sure that they understand the paths to satisfying their own goals. Design those paths in concert with the organization's goals. Marry the two. Show them how they can help the company achieve its goals and simultaneously they will achieve some of theirs.

Employees' self interests are your most powerful lever. When you can align the company's goals with your employees' enlightened self interest, you have the most powerful motivator of all working for you.

TREATING YOUR EMPLOYEES AS YOU WOULD WANT TO BE TREATED
As told by Sid Grosvenor

We've all heard that we should treat others, as we would want to be treated. We all would agree that this is good advice. But, just what does this include?

Usually this means to give them the tools to do the job. Give them legitimate praise. Be accessible and give them feedback on how they're doing. Hold them accountable for their work.

Finally, an important part of treating them, as you would want to be treated is to "Don't play favorites and treat them all the same".

If you're not the CEO, no doubt you will have someone that you must report to, and in large organizations, there may well be standardized performance evaluation forms. So far so good, but what if your employee group feels that the performance responsibilities are just not fair to any of them? This was the situation I had to deal with as a new Sergeant of Police. I had a group of 14 veteran patrol officers to supervise.

At the time, the Patrol Chief had a policy called "Beat Responsibility". This meant that officers assigned to a particular beat had to promptly answer all calls for police service on their beat. They were also held accountable for not preventing crimes that occurred on their beat.

Sounds fair, except that the policy was to count all offenses of whatever type the same and even to count offenses against the beat officer that happened when he was on a prolonged investigation, out of service for hours processing prisoners, or even on a day off. The officers seemed to be doing their best to prevent offenses when and as they could, but they felt that the system was totally unfair.

They rightly complained that their performance evaluations were either good, very good, or bad based as much on luck as how diligent they were in their duties. I agreed with them. I altered the system for the officers under my supervision. Did I have the authority to do so? Frankly, I did not know, but I was being held accountable by my Watch Commander for the offenses that happened so I decided to alter the beat responsibility a bit.

Here's what I did. I simply did not charge an offense against an officer who was not on duty when the offense occurred or who was out of service with a long call for service, or who was processing prisoners when the offense occurred.

It was extra paperwork for me and I was in the office more, even though I preferred to be on the street helping to prevent crimes, covering officers on traffic stops, and responding to important calls. I posted weekly results for my officers so they could see just how they were doing. For the first time since "Beat Responsibility" came into being they felt the system was not just fair, but now it was just.

The extra paper shuffling on my part paid huge dividends. The officers worked harder, because now the hard work counted. All types of offenses took a big dip in my sector. My Watch Commander of course was pleased since the dip in crime made him look good to his Captain, and my own performance evaluation rose accordingly as well.

The Lesson is not just to treat your work group fairly as in "everyone is held to the same standard", but to insure that the "standard is applied in a just way that motivates the entire work group" to achieve peak performance.

Sid Grosvenor was a Police Sergeant in
Dallas, Texas for 35 years and is now a
Buyers Exclusive Realtor at Lake Chapala, Jalisco, Mexico.

"No man will work for your interests unless they are his."
David Seabury

Following up on Napoleon's levers of motivation, we have Seabury's quote on self interest. Understanding human nature and the power of working in concert with it, is a key tool of management.

In Sid's story about the Dallas Police, we see how employees who felt unfairly treated, reacted very negatively to the structure of a performance evaluation program. But when Sid reacted to that and took steps to correct it, he gained both credibility and trust from the patrolmen and started to achieve better results.

The lesson is actually quite simple but, still, it is employed by few. Align the employees self interest with the organization's goals and you can get the results you want. Interact with your people and understand what they want. Each employee will be different but certain themes will hold true for all. Most want nothing more than to be treated fairly and judged impartially. Many want a fair chance to advance and be paid more. Demonstrate to your people that this is possible. Then, like Sid, make it happen.

When holding an employee accountable for results, be sure she agrees that the judgment process is fair as it is constructed. Holding a police officer responsible for events that occurred when he was off duty is difficult to defend. Or holding a teacher responsible for a parent's lack of involvement would seem a stretch. Design your programs with total buy-in and agreement from your employees that the concept is appropriate and fair and then move forward.

Always find a way to include the employee's interests in the process and be sure that as they serve their own interests, they are serving yours too.

SIMON SINEK SPEAKS ABOUT LEADERSHIP

The following is an excerpt from a speech made by Simon Sinek at the TED (Technology, Entertainment, Design) Conference in 2009. We join his presentation as he discusses believing in what you do and communicating that to employees and others:

... But if you don't know why you do what you do, and people respond to why you do what you do, then how will you ever get people to vote for you, or buy something from you, or, more importantly, be loyal and want to be a part of what it is that you do. Again, the goal is not just to sell to people who need what you have; the goal is to sell to people who believe what you believe. The goal is not just to hire people who need a job; it's to hire people who believe what you believe. I always say that, you know, if you hire people just because they can do a job, they'll work for your money, but if you hire people who believe what you believe, they'll work for you with blood and sweat and tears.

People don't buy what you do; they buy why you do it. And if you talk about what you believe, you will attract those who believe what you believe.

So let me give you a famous example, a famous failure and a famous success of the law of diffusion of innovation. First, the famous failure. It's a commercial example. As we said before, a second ago, the recipe for success is money and the right people and the right market conditions, right? You should have success then. Look at TiVo. From the time TiVo came out about eight or nine years ago to this current day, they are the single highest-quality product on the market, hands down, there is no dispute. They were extremely well-funded. Market conditions were fantastic. I mean, we use TiVo as a verb. I TiVo stuff on my piece of junk Time Warner DVR all the time.

But TiVo's a commercial failure. They've never made money. And when they went IPO, their stock was at about 30 or 40 dollars and then plummeted, and it's never traded above 10. In fact, I don't think it's even traded above six, except for a couple of little spikes. Because you see, when TiVo launched their product they told us all what they had. They said, "We have a product that pauses live TV, skips commercials, rewinds live TV and memorizes your viewing habits without you even asking." And the cynical majority said, "We don't believe you. We don't need it. We don't like it. You're scaring us." What if they had said, "If you're the kind of person who likes to have total control over every aspect of your life, boy, do we have a product for you. It pauses live TV, skips commercials, memorizes your viewing habits, etc., etc." People don't buy what you do; they buy why you do it, and what you do simply serves as the proof of what you believe.

Now let me give you a successful example of the law of diffusion of innovation. In the summer of 1963, 250,000 people showed up on the mall in Washington to hear Dr. King speak. They sent out no invitations, and there was no website to check the date. How do you do that? Well, Dr. King wasn't the only man in America who was a great orator. He wasn't the only man in America who suffered in a pre-civil rights America. In fact, some of his ideas were bad. But he had a gift. He didn't go around telling people what needed to change in America. He went around and told people what he believed. "I believe, I believe, I believe," he told people. And people who believed what he believed took his cause, and they made it their own, and they told people. And some of those people created structures to get the word out to even more people. And lo and behold, 250,000 people showed up on the right day at the right time to hear him speak. How many of them showed up for him? Zero. They showed up for themselves. It's what they believed about America that got them to travel in a bus for eight hours to stand in the sun in Washington in the middle of August. It's what they believed, and it wasn't about black versus white: 25 percent of the audience was white. Dr. King believed that there are two types of laws in this world: those that are made by a higher authority and those that are made by man. And not until all the laws that are made by man are consistent with the laws that are made by the higher authority will we live in a just world. It just so happened that the Civil Rights Movement was the perfect thing to help him bring his cause to life. We followed, not for him, but for ourselves. And, by the way, he gave the "I have a dream" speech, not the "I have a plan" speech.

Listen to politicians now, with their comprehensive 12-point plans. They're not inspiring anybody. Because there are leaders and there are those who lead. Leaders hold a position of power or authority, but those who lead inspire us. **Whether they're individuals or organizations, we follow those who lead, not because we have to, but because we want to. We follow those who lead, not for them, but for ourselves. And it's those who start with "why" that have the ability to inspire those around them or find others who inspire them.**

For more information on Simon Sinek, visit his website at www.startwithwhy.com. The entire speech by Simon Sinek is available on YouTube at http://www.ted.com/talks/simon_sinek_how_great_leaders_inspire_action.html

"If you have a lot of cash you want to get rid of and want to create entitlements for your people, implement a profit sharing program."
Robert Papes

Profit Sharing! What a noble concept! Who could ever say anything bad about that? Both this author and Mr. Papes believe that as a motivational tool, profit sharing is a fantastic way to throw your money away.

Sharing profits with the employees is a fine idea if your goal is to give a gift to your people. It has been touted as a way to get everyone to care about controlling costs and making right decisions. But, unfortunately, with very few exceptions, it does not motivate.

A company's profits are mostly affected by the state of the economy in general, industry trends, business cycles, senior management's direction and the luck of the draw. A mail clerk's ability to affect company-wide profits is best described as slim to none. And, even if he were to find a way to somehow improve the bottom line, his share of the reward is so watered down that it goes unnoticed.

To truly motivate through a cash incentive, the program has to be geared to that individual's job, fairly calculated to account for profit, objectively counted, simple to understand and paid on a timely basis. Paying a Profit Share bonus once per year never has and never will motivate the rank and file. It is a fine gesture and gift but it has two drawbacks: First, as stated, it fails to motivate and second, it becomes viewed as an entitlement that the employees are owed. Entitlements do not motivate, they sour with age and invariably disappoint people.

To motivate your crew, tie their bonuses to their specific performance and pay it frequently enough to make them think about it every day.

SUMMARY:

Building an effective compensation system should include some form of incentive pay. Avoid paying the employee all of their pay for showing up each day. Tie a portion (potentially 10 to 25%) to performance not promises.

- Expect specific performance levels by each employee. Clearly define the goals and then reward results that are above and beyond normal levels.
- Remember that you can reward in many ways. Make use of recognition, appropriate praise, and advancements as tools but never forget that cash makes the world go round and money is how we keep score.
- Strive for consistency in all your dealings.
- Embrace employees' self interest and align their goals with the company's objectives. With everyone on the same page, results come faster and easier.
- Never forget that people will work with you because you and your organization stand for something that fills a need for them. Trusting you and believing in what you do and WHY you do it, is what draws high quality work out of your employees.

One of the beauties of a well designed bonus program is that it provides built-in reinforcement in the form of timely bonus payouts. But your people will need one-on-one coaching and formal reviews as well. And those must be done properly. The next step is radical so keep an open mind and then de-link.

CHAPTER SIX

DELINK AND REVIEW

"So how much do I get!?"
My employee

Somewhere along the line, a tradition began. Somehow, American business collectively decided that it was a good policy to give an annual performance review to each employee and couple that with a discussion of their compensation. Usually that meant a raise of some kind for the employee or a conversation about why their pay would remain constant as is. Rarely did it ever mean a decrease in pay.

And that was it. That was the accepted process for giving non-union employees feedback and pay adjustments.

This falls under the category of 'it seemed like a good idea at the time'. It WAS a good idea. Fifty years ago. It was far better than no performance review and no raises. But it also falls into that same bucket load of methods we use because we have always done it that way. Sometimes, old processes need to be dusted off and analyzed. Sometimes we have to adapt to our changing world and do something different.

Today's Annual Review is a stressful, scary and life-changing event that has very little to do with communication and very much to do with making or breaking careers. It is an antiquated process that demands rethinking.

DELINK AND PROSPER

This was the 257th performance review I had given at my delivery company and I was in rare form. I was flying along in record speed, hitting the highlights, skipping past the boring stuff, glossing over the unimportant. I told this young man what I felt he was doing well and on what I thought he needed to improve. Then I got to the part that tied it all together and reinforced my decision on the size of his raise. It was all very well thought out and delivered with precision. With all this practice, I had really learned to communicate effectively.

Except that I hadn't. Communicated, that is. I realized later that while I was telling him the specifics of his review; while I was praising his strong points and detailing his weaker problem areas; he was never really listening. All he could think about was whether or not he was going to get as big a raise as he expected. Because that was the way it worked. You sit patiently through your review and then, at the end, when the blowhard manager gets tired of hearing his own voice, you will find out how much you get.

Performance reviews are difficult enough without adding the extra burden of matching the "tone" of your review with the size of the raise. Giving a good review requires attentiveness by both parties, serious discussion and the presence of mind to be "in the moment". My reviews had none of those things.

And so it was that on my 258th review, I changed procedures. OK, honestly, I don't know what number review it was ... but it was probably pretty close to that. After some discussions with my management team, we decided to make a serious break from tradition and re-think everything we believed about performance reviews and raises. That was when we decided to 'Delink and Prosper'.

It started with a memo to all the employees followed by a one on one conversation with each. We explained that from that point onward, we would no longer be coupling the annual review with an annual pay raise.

There would still be reviews but they would just be give-and-take discussions ... not a prelude to a raise. We told everyone that from now on, pay raises would be periodic as deserved. The raises would probably be gradual, smaller and more frequent but there was no maximum or minimum set. We emphasized that although longevity of employment was valued, it was not a primary determinant of raise frequency or size. We were evolving into a true meritocracy.

At first many employees did not believe us. They assumed it was a cloaked way to cut costs. That slowly changed as we demonstrated that raises would happen intermittently (more on that later) as individual performance demanded.

There were some surprising and fascinating repercussions to this policy. Some folks who seemed to always "raise their game" just before review time suddenly started performing more strongly each day. Reviews became far less stressful for everyone. Now instead of it being a crucial career making (or breaking) moment, they became a quality conversation about how the employee can improve to gain future pay increases. And giving out a raise turned into a fun experience. We would, without warning, pull an employee into the office and tell them matter-of-factly that they were doing well and we were bumping their hourly rate up X cents. There were no expectations to meet or exceed; just the joy of getting a surprise raise and turning an ordinary day into a special one.

Successfully implementing the Delink and Prosper plan requires systematic management oversight of each employee's performance, a genuine commitment to raising pay appropriately and not abusing the system to save on costs. I found this process to be a re-energizing approach to managing my company and a key step to creating the ultimate motivated employee.

GB

"There are two things people want more than sex and money ... recognition and praise."
                                    Mary Kay Ash

  Mary Kay Ash built her cosmetics business on a philosophy of respect for her employees. Out of virtually nothing, she built a multi-million dollar enterprise that thrived because it combined opportunity with motivation.

  Her comment that recognition and praise were more important than sex and money, may have been designed to be controversial and attention getting. But her point went to the very essence of humanity. It addressed that deep crying need in every one of us to be noticed and appreciated.

  In a business sense, the lesson is no less significant. Paying more to workers only goes so far. Have you ever had a friend who held a high paying job? Perhaps you envied them just a little bit. And when they leave that job and you ask them why, their answer is rarely that they were unhappy about their pay. No, it's always something personal. They weren't respected or recognized fully for their contributions. They didn't feel appreciated. And after they are done, you likely still think to yourself *"Yeah, but what about all that money ..."*

  When you interact with your employees, particularly in performance reviews, be sure to find something they do that you can be thankful for and tell them how much you appreciate it. Accent the positive before discussing the areas that need improvement. Finish off those conversations with a return to the positives. Ken Blanchard observed that *"It takes a four to one positive to negative ratio, for a manager to be perceived as a positive manager."* Yes, money motivates but recognition and praise is what keeps them showing up and trying harder.

SHE NEVER SAW IT COMING ...

She was a waif of a girl, not much over 21 and with very little experience. Heather, my Customer Service Manager, interviewed her, liked her, and decided to hire her as one of our Customer Service Agents. Her name was Nicole and we had high hopes for her.

Life had not exactly been easy for Nicole. She had a series of difficult experiences that would have stifled a weaker spirit's enthusiasm for life. But she was strong of heart and embraced her new job and everything about it. Heather started her on the three day training course. With calls coming in rapid fire, we liked to break people in slowly. Most trainees needed three to five days before going 'solo'.

Nicole took all of three hours to learn the ropes. She was a natural on the phone and quick and nimble on the keyboard. She started fast and sped up from there.

A short time later, Heather came into my office and said, *"Gary, Nicole is doing really well."*

"That's nice" I replied.

"No, I mean she is doing really, really well!"

Heather wasn't one for over-dramatizing things so now she had my attention. She suggested we give Nicole an early 5% raise. It was modest but we had never raised anyone that fast before. We normally waited until the probation period was over and then proceeded cautiously.

So Heather gave Nicole an informal review and finished with, *"Nicole, you've done so well in your short time here that you've forced us to raise you up 50 cents an hour, effective last week on the first."* Then she smiled and said, *"Thank you."*

Nicole seemed stunned. She was beaming. Later, she told us it surprised her to get a raise that fast and motivated her more to keep on improving. Heather saw a huge training success. I saw the power of timely, smaller and more frequent raises for good performance. And Nicole, well, she never saw it coming ...

GB

> "People often say that motivation doesn't last. Well, neither does bathing – that's why we recommend it daily."
>
> Zig Ziglar

Zig was on to something here. And if anyone knew something about motivation, it was Mr. Ziglar.

This thought brings us back to the fact that motivation is not to be thought of as a single act or a random event. To truly be effective, building a motivated work force is an on-going business philosophy that permeates every action you take. It is creating the basic proper atmosphere for a motivated crew to work in; it is hiring and training the right staff; it is rewarding and giving feedback properly and consistently.

So you may ask, *"Even if I develop that motivating ambience and believe all the rest, how do I keep it going every day?"* As Zig stated, you do it daily. You demonstrate to your people that you can walk the walk not just talk the talk. You watch for opportunities to give genuine praise and you seize them. You review your staff pay rates weekly and ask yourself if anyone is ready for a bump up. You do those things that reinforce the belief that those who work hard, reap rewards. When your workers believe that you will notice, appreciate and reward consistently, your credibility will rise just as the productivity does.

In Nicole's case, it wasn't the size of the raise that overwhelmed her. Surely, fifty cents per hour was not a lifestyle changer. What surprised and delighted her was the fact that management noticed and responded far faster than she expected. That immediately made our company different from others at which she had worked. What we did, reinforced what we had told her we would do. And the value of that is immeasurable.

Daily reaffirmation through deeds and action is what renders results.

> **"Part of courage is simple consistency."**
> Peggy Noonan

At first, this does not sound like a remarkable quote. It is very short and seems sort of mundane. So, now consistency is some kind of great virtue? What's next? Praising the art of being boring or routine or indistinguishable from others?

But what Ms. Noonan has done is capture an elusive truth in a brief stroke. Consistency in life and in business is under rated and unappreciated. Until you are the one who needs someone else to be consistent. Then, suddenly, it becomes very important.

It DOES take courage to be consistent. Ever had a customer who paid 'full boat' but got poor service? When a customer like that complains, wouldn't you give them a discount or refund? What happens when they don't complain? Do you offer it anyway? Or does courage take a day off so you can pad your bank account? Life is full of those choices and it is hard to always take the high road.

However, in dealing with your employees, consistency is one of the greatest virtues and that requires courage too. If the stated penalty for a specific mistake is a one-day suspension, do you always administer that in the same way for all employees? What if Sue, your star employee, made that error? Would she still get a day off? Courage is a necessary component to consistency. And when your employees see it demonstrated, you are reinforcing the rules and the norm.

In today's world, courage is usually associated with acts of heroism; with single momentary events of drama. But who would you admire most: The ne'er-do-well that pulls a victim from a burning car or the mother who works every day of her life to care for her disabled child?

"When I get a review, I can never understand the difference between FAIR and AVERAGE."
My employee

Quality is a key component of every product. No one ever says *"I don't care about quality."* And yet, as managers, we often fail to give a performance review of truly high standards.

There are many forms available for performance reviews and many companies create their own versions. It is good to tailor your reviews specifically to an individual employee's function rather than to use a one-size-fits-all approach.

It is better still to offer multiple reviews frequently so that your people get constant feedback. That is one reason that higher frequency bonus programs have more success. When the bonus period runs for only thirty days, the employee gets feedback constantly on their performance and cash reinforcement as well. In that way, monthly bonuses actually act as an impartial and objective review process.

But when giving what is considered a 'formal review', using the right format and giving clear cut specifics is far more motivating than general comments. For example, rating someone on a scale of 1 to 10 on specific aspects of their job provides more quality feedback than saying that they are doing a fair job or an average one. Although a score of 5 might be the same as 'average' it also has the advantage of being specific. It's a 5, not a 4 or 6. This gives the employee something specific to aim for on the next review. If their average score is 5.7, then you, as manager, may be able to say, *"When that gets over 6.2, we'll be talking about a raise."*

Be specific. Give high quality feedback and expect results.

10,000 PECKING PIGEONS CAN'T BE WRONG

In a study published by Pearson in 2009, four Psychology Professors analyzed the four recognized schedules of reinforcement. They are:
- Fixed Ratio: reinforcement after a consistent number of correct responses.
- Fixed Interval: reinforcement after a specific period of time has elapsed.
- Variable Ratio: reinforce after a specific number of correct responses on average.
- Variable Interval: reinforcement for correct responses after an average time interval, with the actual interval varying randomly.

The study primarily used pigeons pecking at a target. Depending on which schedule was being used, the pigeons were reinforced with a pellet of food. The number and frequency of pecks was tracked by computer and the results were posted graphically.

When it came to motivating the pigeons to peck, one method far exceeded all of the others in effectiveness. Variable Interval was found to be many times more effective than the other three schedules.

When deciding on how to give raises, keep this in mind. For example, using a Fixed Ratio schedule might mean giving a call order taker a raise every 5,000 calls handled. Fixed Interval would mean a raise every six months. Variable Ratio might result in a raise every 4,000 to 6,000 calls. But Variable Interval means the raise could come at any time <u>as performance dictates</u>.

The latter method nets higher results consistently. When your employees believe that any day or any one action done well could result in an instant pay raise, the dynamics of your workplace change dramatically. And we know that is true ... because 10,000 pecking pigeons can't be wrong.

"Social interactions are the greatest source of intermittent reinforcement in human behavior."
                    Fester and Culbertson
                    Behavior Principles

Sporadic and intermittent reinforcement is the most powerful tool available for motivating employees. It can come in the form of promotions, bonuses, raises, extra perks, recognition or perhaps just a simple 'atta-boy'.

But of all these delivery methods, none is more powerful than those that focus on human interaction. Getting a well timed pat on the back (figuratively or literally) can often be more motivating than an extra fifty dollars on a paycheck.

As managers of people, we must never underestimate the power of our own influence. Taking a few private moments to chat or interact with your employees and sharing some genuine appreciation for their efforts can spur people on to better and better effort. Just as getting recognition in front of your peers for a job well done can encourage an employee to work harder to 'live up' to their new sterling reputation.

Be smart. Use all the arrows in your quiver. Aim carefully and make full use of the greatest levers for action at your disposal. Intermittent reinforcement via personal interaction with your employees can net incredible results.

MAXIMIZE THE IMPACT

Sharon had not been with the company very long. She started as a Customer Service Agent for us in August and now, three months later, she was very acclimated and doing quite well. In the courier business, the calls come in to our dispatch center in fairly rapid action and sometimes it's all we can do to keep up with them. New hires tend to be a bit overwhelmed with the fast pace and the challenge of taking one call after another and maintaining their composure.

This one Tuesday had been a bit of a wild one. Sharon had already taken 34 calls and it was only 10am. And, of course, virtually every call was a frenzied receptionist who wanted to give us all the information on her next delivery in one breath. Sharon was keeping pace and holding her own.

That's when it happened. I was walking through the Dispatch office just observing when I could tell that Sharon had a call unlike the others. It was a miffed customer. Something had not gone right with her delivery and she was letting us have it with both barrels. I could only hear Sharon's part of the conversation but I have been on the receiving end of enough of those to imagine quite accurately what she was hearing. So, I stayed back and watched Sharon handle this upset customer.

It was like watching Michelangelo carving the marble David; like Peyton Manning finding the open receiver; like JFK delivering an inspirational speech. Somewhere from within, this young lady rose to the occasion and summoned all her diplomatic powers. She defused the situation like a professional. First she let the customer vent, then she asked a few simple questions to make sure she understood the problem. She agreed with the customer that the service we provided left something to be desired, and she apologized. She agreed, without delay, to deduct all the charges for the delivery and then asked if there was anything else she could do to smooth things over with that customer's client. Finally she closed with another apology and informed the customer that she would be passing the information on to the Management team so they could analyze what happened and decrease the odds that it would ever happen again.

I mean, it was like textbook perfect. We train people to follow those general steps but rarely is it done well. Even I get flustered when an angry customer calls and I struggle to handle the situation properly. Anyway, about ten minutes after she took the call, I asked her to step into my office. She was a bit nervous about that request but I tried to put her at ease immediately. I had her sit down and, sincerely, I looked directly at her and said, *"Sharon, I heard your end of that complaint call today. And I just wanted to tell you that I have never heard anyone handle an irate customer as well as you did today. You let them vent, you didn't disagree, you took immediate action, I'm telling you, it was perfect and I am so happy you are a part of our team. And, I called you in because it is action like that which makes me realize you need to be paid more. It's a small thing but I am bumping your pay up from $6 to $6.50 per hour"* (yup, this was quite some time ago ...).

Sharon was a bit taken aback but the smile on her face told me she was pleased. I emphasized how much we valued her and that her pay level was largely in her hands. Doing well made her more valuable to the company and it made us more motivated to keep her here. Rewarding correct action on the spot increases the odds that it will occur more frequently. Maximize your opportunities to reinforce positive actions and you will start changing your Corporate Culture for the better.

GB

> "Catch someone doing something right."
> Kenneth Blanchard & Spencer Johnson

Five brief words summarizing a potent yet often unused management tool; so simple, so elegant and so insightful. Blanchard and Johnson were commenting on a clever tactic that is well overlooked.

Catch someone doing something right! So often, we are focused on the opposite; pointing out errors, being critical, micro-managing and responding to the negatives in life. Try the opposite for a while.

The beauty of this concept is so subtle it is often unnoticed. But, once again, it goes back to both the use of intermittent reinforcement and the maximizing of leverage via personal interaction. Catching someone in the act of doing something well can give you the opportunity to reinforce correct behavior so that it is repeated and to react with a motivating raise or other action to show you are walking the walk.

And it is so easy! People do things right all day long every day. Pick a moment when any act was done exceptionally well and recognize it. Public recognition is best because you are influencing everyone rather than just the doer of the deed. And reinforcing the action with a positive reaction increases your credibility and influence.

But, finally, a word of caution: Reacting to one deed done well must not look contrived or too random. Rewards should be given for exemplary efforts and all praise should be genuine and heartfelt. If the employees believe that it is given cavalierly or with random abandon, the impact is lost. Simply shift your focus on watching for a job truly well done and seize the chance to react positively when it is merited.

"The most basic of all human needs is the need to understand and be understood. The best way to understand people is to <u>listen</u> to them."

Ralph Nichols

Have you ever had an employee come into your office and ramble a bit as they tried to share their thoughts with you? What did you do? Did you cut them off and indicate your time was short? Did you argue with them and prove that you were right and they were wrong? Or did you listen?

As we discussed before, listening, truly listening, is a lost art form. Our time seems so valuable and we all feel pressured to make something useful out of each minute that taking the time to listen seems like a wasteful expenditure.

It is not. Never has been. Are there limits to how long you can spend listening? Of course. And naturally, some occasions are inappropriate or untimely. But, listening to an employee is not, in and of itself, a waste of time.

The next time an employee wants to come in and share a thought with you, relax and exercise your will to listen. People will feel that you are respectful of them and their efforts when you listen without judgment or rebuke. And listen for what they are really saying. Try to fathom the real reason they have come to you to talk. It is not always about the topic they are discussing. In short, let them ramble and tell you in their own way.

The key to listening well is to realize you are not obligated to agree with them. You may well agree but it's also likely you do not. It doesn't matter. Listening is about respecting and valuing their opinion for what it is. When you remove the burden you feel about your need to 'win the argument' or sway someone's opinion in the opposite direction, you give yourself permission to listen without judgment. Just do it, and then close by saying *"Those are well thought out points. I'll ponder on them."*

It's easy to show respect. Just listen.

SUMMARY:

Motivating your people succeeds best when you can recognize and reward appropriately. More frequent rewarding has more power to influence. Use all the levers at your disposal.

- Delink annual performance reviews from the raise decision process. Make the review process more of a give-and-take where together you are discussing the ways that the employee can help the company succeed while meeting their own objectives too.
- Review with precision. Make sure your review message is not obscured by the use of ambiguous phrases. Give people a number score in applicable areas so that they have specific targets for improvement.
- Be consistent in both your discipline and your rewards. Your power and influence increase when you are in harmony with past actions and are perceived to be <u>dependably predictable</u>.
- Maximize the use of intermittent reinforcement. Organize yourself so that you track the dates of each employee's last raise and review their status frequently to determine if they are due again. Frequent, smaller and timely raises given for quality work are far more effective than annual 'gift' raises.
- Catch someone doing something right. Seek to accent the positive instead of always pointing out errors. Remember, to be viewed as a supportive and positive manager, you must have at least a 4 to 1 positive to negative action ratio.

Creating a team of truly motivated employees requires dedication and a unique focus on all your interpersonal actions. Your job will be easier if the employees have the strong sense that you are in their corner and care about their well being. A sure way to demonstrate that is by Servant Leadership.

CHAPTER SEVEN

BE THE SERVANT

"And whosoever of you will be the chiefest, shall be the servant of all."

                        King James Version: Mark 10:44

Are you a leader or a boss? And how do you know the difference?

Have you ever worked with someone that you fully relied on? Someone who always seemed to know the right thing to do and was always there for you? Where would you go when you needed help? Who would you turn to when your path was not clear? That same person. Every time. And whether you recognized it or not, whether she had the title or not, that person was your leader.

A leader is someone who cares about others and does their best to help them. He or she gives them the tools to do their job, the light to see their way clearly and the extra push in the right direction. A leader is a servant of others, and, paradoxically, that is what gives him or her the power.

So in your quest to motivate people and rise to greater and greater heights, seek only to help others do their job; seek ways to clear their path and brighten it for them; seek to assist them in their journey to do the best job possible. For that is what will set you apart from others and that 'Be the Servant' attitude will instill your voice with authority that resonates.

LEADERS MUST CARE

Leadership is about people. Period. Great Leadership is about inspiring people, serving people, caring for people, caring <u>about</u> people. You have to tell them you care.

We assembled a panel of Southwest Employees who had heroically served our country in the Iraq war, to address our Leadership. We asked them to describe what great Leadership looked like to them. No one told tales of how smart their Leaders were. No one cared where their Leader was from, or what was on their Leader's resume. To a soldier, their heroes were the ones who cared about them—as human beings, as well as soldiers. Their Leaders worked them hard, disciplined them when necessary, and sent them into battle! Yet, these soldiers knew, without a doubt, that their Leaders cared for each soldier's total well-being. Somehow, some way, you have to convince people you care about them. And, in turn, your people will be ready to help you win great battles.

Southwest is a great company in a very difficult industry. Southwest is known for excellence in many categories, including Customer Service, operations, and financial performance. I'm most proud, though, that we've been able to take care of our People.

From a speech delivered by Gary Kelly,
Southwest Airlines Chairman, at the University of Texas
Commencement Ceremonies in 2010.

"You can observe a lot just by watching."

Yogi Berra

"Hard work spotlights the character of people: some turn up their sleeves, some turn up their noses, and some don't turn up at all."

Sam Ewig

There are two schools of thought here and both have a tinge of truth to them.

Years ago there was a business philosophy that was nicknamed 'Management by walking around' and it had its share of adherents. The concept was simply that part of the day should be devoted to observing and watching the business process in action. This, in itself, is a very valid process. For a perceptive viewer, much could be gained from that. If you don't already do that, try just watching and observing how the work process flows.

However another method that tends to gain more employee trust and respect is fairly the opposite of walking around. Simply stated, it is rolling up your sleeves and doing the work yourself. It is the proverbial 'getting your hands dirty' as you perform specific lower level functions on your own. It is a team building experience that reaps benefits for the long term.

You have seen it yourself. When you jumped in and answered calls for orders alongside the office crew; when you helped load the truck so a driver could leave on time; when you made a sales call with your rep and closed the deal. Nothing means more to the vast range of employees than seeing the boss do the same work they do.

Yogi didn't have much to prove. He had been an All-star catcher for years so when he managed ballplayers, they already knew what he could do. You are not Yogi. Get dirty. Prove you not only expect others to do the work, but you are always ready to do it yourself.

THE SOLDIERS IN THE TRENCH

The story goes that sometime, close to a battlefield over 200 years ago, a man in civilian clothes rode past a small group of exhausted battle-weary soldiers digging an obviously important defensive position. The section leader, making no effort to help, was shouting orders, threatening punishment if the work was not completed within the hour.

"Why are you are not helping?" asked the stranger on horseback.

"I am in charge. The men do as I tell them," said the section leader, adding, "Help them yourself if you feel strongly about it."

To the section leader's surprise the stranger dismounted and helped the men until the job was finished.

Before leaving the stranger congratulated the men for their work, and approached the puzzled section leader. "You should notify top command next time your rank prevents you from supporting your men - and I will provide a more permanent solution," said the stranger.

Up close, the section leader now recognized General Washington, and also the lesson he'd just been taught.

A true parable about leadership? We may never know, but if the story is not true, certainly the lesson is.

Reprinted with permission from www.businessballs.com, a website dedicated to offering a free ethical learning and development resource for people and organizations, run by Alan Chapman, in Leicester, England

"Credibility is like virginity. Once you lose it, you can never get it back."

Unknown

If you have ever been there, you already understand. Credibility lost, especially with employees or your superiors, is never found again. The repercussions of lost credibility follow you in your career for all your days.

Is there a magic pill you can swallow that will save you from this terrible curse of lost credibility? Amazingly there is, but it is often a bitter pill and one that no one wants to swallow. It is truth, introspection and honesty.

Now, none of us sets out purposely on a path that requires deceit and duplicity to succeed. And no manager should expect that they will be saint-like and never succumb to the temptation to twist the truth a little when circumstances make that an appealing solution. No one is ever perfect but a modest failure now and then does not destroy credibility. Your integrity is defined by what you do in the most important of situations. It is then, that giving in to the well traveled road of untruthfulness will put you in danger of losing that which you cannot ever gain back.

The pill you have to swallow whole is the capsule of truth. If there is a major setback and someone must take the heat, a leader with integrity steps up and tells the truth, even if that truth points to them as the origin of the failure. You ask your employees to recognize their own faults and failures, so you must do so as well. This is why being humble pays dividends. Those not laden with the yoke of perfection can more easily accept their own hand in a failure. Telling the truth and accepting responsibility is the elixir that saves you in the end.

WHEN ALL ELSE FAILS, WRITE IT DOWN ...

It was Friday afternoon, the tenth of April. I had just finished a difficult performance review with Wes. I closed it by reminding him of the key steps he needed to take to improve specific skills and then telling him that I would be watching his performance. I also told him that I would watch for ninety days and then we would talk again.

It hadn't been a really pleasant meeting. Wes disagreed strongly with my assessment but he handled it maturely and returned to his station to continue that day's work. I made a few notes to myself and then placed his review into his file.

To his credit, Wes actually made some special efforts and began to improve those weak areas that were holding him back. His interpersonal relations with the other office folks became smoother and he fine tuned his understanding of the computer system. It seemed like our discussion was having the desired effect.

Summer rolled around and suddenly it was July. On the morning of the tenth of July, I looked at my desk calendar and noticed a note to myself: "90 days for Wes" was all it said. That was enough to jar my memory. The day, however, flew by and it wasn't until 4pm that I decided I had better follow through.

I went up to Wes's work station and said, *"Wes, can you stop by my office and see me before you leave tonight?"*

To my immense surprise, Wes lit up and beamed back at me. *"I thought you'd forget!"* he said. And that was when I realized how many times in the past I **had** forgotten. I didn't realize that the employee is taking me at my word and he is counting the days too! Credibility can be won with the stroke of a pen. Keeping your promises is a key to maintaining motivation.

GB

"The more you are willing to accept responsibility for your actions, the more credibility you will have."
                              Brian Koslow

It is a bitter pill. All of us would like to be able to say that we have been huge successes in whatever field we are in. Having to admit that sometimes we have been on the losing end of a game is not enjoyable.

Interestingly, the problem is not so much an issue of integrity as it is of process. That is, many business managers simply don't know how to do it. How do you admit failure and yet retain your authority?

The solution is to step outside of yourself. Pretend that you are an uninterested observer and are analyzing a series of events to see how and why something went wrong. Don't focus on who is to blame. Focus on the process that occurred as the failure unfolded. As you do that, you will soon see a key moment in time when the seeds of failure were planted. You will discover a fundamental error of judgment that led you and others down the wrong path. Use that knowledge as a teaching point.

There is no shame in failure. There is only shame in not having the will to try at all. You tried. Give yourself credit for that. You failed. Give yourself forgiveness for that too. Then maximize the benefits by identifying the lesson learned and share that with others. Admitting that you erred is acknowledging that you are human. There is no crime there. Covering it up or blaming someone else is when you've lost the true value of the event.

When you can discuss the course of events with detached professionalism and admit your share of the errors, you set an example for all of your employees to follow. Your superiors will already be one step ahead of you and will applaud your willingness to learn from the situation.

Step outside yourself and be a pro about it.

SERVANT LEADERSHIP

By Harry Tucker

In recent years, the notion of servant leadership has become popular, promoting the idea of the selfless leader who serves others, who raises others to new heights and who helps others be the best that they can be. Above all, they do it naturally. It is, after all, something that is a part of who they are.

While many people have humbled me with the moniker of servant leader, I remind them that if I have seen further, it is because I have stood on the shoulders of giants, as so eloquently said by Sir Isaac Newton. I am inspired to serve by servant leaders who are far better than I.

Servant Leadership manifests itself in different forms. Sometimes it is the business manager who plays more of a role as a visionary and facilitator than a boss. Servant leaders don't rule over others even if title suggests they should, but instead serve the needs of those who work for them; casting the vision, removing obstacles and creating connections that enable people to rise to their ultimate potential and contribution personally and professionally.

Some years ago, a gentleman by the name of Narender Nath worked for me at the software company that I had cofounded in New York. Narender was a gentle soul who laughed easily and laughed much. He was fascinated by American culture (having grown up in India) and believed that television commercials were a powerful insight into that culture. So when many of us were getting up for snacks during a commercial break, that was when Narender was sitting down to pay attention to the commercials.

We held an internal corporate chess tournament for fun and while Narender did not know how to play, he asked me to teach him the rules. Many of us in the tournament were expert class or better and Narender was soundly trounced in every game. Despite his poor performance, he was delighted with participating and I once remarked that I was impressed at how well he carried himself when many people would be frustrated or angry at the humiliating result. He indicated that the only reason he played was for the camaraderie with others, the opportunity to learn something new and the opportunity to get to know people better. The game was merely the conduit for the connection, the connection being more important than winning or losing a game. I discovered then that he was wise as well as gentle.

Narender was taken from us on 9/11, being on the impact floor of the North Tower of the World Trade Center.

When the time came to have our annual chess tournament, most of the guys didn't want to participate because they felt it wouldn't be the same without Narender. I thought about it for a bit and thought "Narender wouldn't have wanted it to end this way". So I suggested that we have a pay-to-play tournament, with a minimum $25 to play and the admission fees divided up among selected charities.

What followed next humbled and amazed me. People paid hundreds to play, with most of them naming children's charities. In the years that followed, the tournament expanded to include players who were not members of our company, resulting in thousands of dollars being donated to children's charities.

In the last few years, many of us have moved on, being busy with Life and being scattered around the world and sadly, the tournament hasn't been held for a couple of years.

Many people who have learned about the tournament often cite the creation of the tournament as an example of my servant leadership, inspiring people to do greater things for others despite adversity. Others have copied this tournament and cited the story of Narender as their source of inspiration.

I believe in this case that Narender is the real servant leader. In life, he taught us to be a better human being, to see the best in everyone and to make the best out of every situation.

And in true servant leader fashion, even when he is no longer with us, his legacy of doing the best you can while serving and helping others continues to inspire many to make a difference in the world. And like the wise business leader, he influenced not by edict, but by example.

That is the legacy of a true servant leader.

Harry has provided strategy and global enterprise technology architecture guidance to Wall Street and Fortune 25 companies for over 25 years. He also specializes in the area of predictive analytics, co-founding an award-winning software company in New York that specialized in human capital optimization; capturing and expressing human productivity mathematically. He can be reached at his website at www.harrytucker.com.

"As we look into the next century, leaders will be those who empower others."
Bill Gates

Several business giants have expressed essentially the same thought but Gates said it succinctly.

A boss consolidates and keeps power within his grasp. A leader delegates, supports and empowers. True success on a larger level comes from working through others not from controlling them. And you can work through them more efficiently when you give them the tools to do their job. And one of those tools is power.

We have all worked for someone who insists that you will be given the power to solve problems or take action, only to find out that no such power has been given at all. Bosses who withhold that power believe that they are the ones who need to be pulling all the strings and that their managers are puppets who do their bidding. Small organizations can function that way but greatness will never be their reward.

Incredible, nearly magical company success comes from a team of motivated, inspired, engaged, independent thinkers empowered by their leader to 'go forth and do good'. True leaders give their people not only the power to make decisions but also all the tools to follow through. And, yes, that same leader exercises their right to receive timely updates and have input into the process to make sure all is moving in the proper direction. But, first, she grants the power to others to affect change.

Again, paradoxically, having the ability to release power to others only increases your own. Ask Bill.

SUMMARY:

The lesson here is simple but essential. Strength of leadership is earned through your actions. Make them the right ones.

- Be the servant of others. Focus on employees and help them help the company. Provide support. Do not be overly concerned about your 'station'. This isn't about you. This is about making your organization successful and that happens through the efforts of all your people. Your job is to support them.
- Roll up your sleeves now and then and pitch in. Walk the walk and show that your concern is for getting the job done, not protecting your status.
- Guard your credibility with real ferocity. Accept responsibility for errors and spread the praise for success. Lead not by edict but by example and show your people that trying hard but failing is not shameful. Own your errors and your credibility will always remain intact.
- Let go of power. One of the hardest lessons of management is how to release authority and empower others. Retain proper controls but trust and respect your people enough to give them the tools they need to effectively do their jobs.
- Finally, seek out what you can do for your employees that is not necessarily part of the employment contract. Listen to their dreams, make note of their desires. Connect them with others who can help or counsel them as they need it. Help them make a difference too.

You have laid the groundwork. You have now made all the right moves and are almost done. The only thing left to do is make sure that everyone is respected, involved and given the chance to contribute in their own way.

CHAPTER EIGHT

RESPECT AND INVOLVE

"Respect a man, he will do the more."
James Howell

Howell says it all. A man or woman's station in life, no matter how exalted, should never justify treating another person poorly. However failing to have respect for others is a common fault of many business managers and needs to be addressed.

During your typical business day, you will always have multiple interactions with employees working directly for you or with others who are below you in the pecking order. If you harbor any feelings of disrespect for those people, it is extremely hard to disguise them. In fact, any employee will pick up on those negative vibrations and recognize them for what they are.

So if there is no disguising your feelings, what can you do? Clearly, the only solution is to have a heart-to-heart chat with yourself and find some way to purge those feelings from your soul. Many educated managers feel that they are 'better' than their underlings. But by the true definition of the word, they are not. They may be more educated, perhaps smarter or funnier or healthier or taller; but that does not make them 'better'. If you sense that you feel superior and cannot hide it, remind yourself that you may be many things in comparison to your employee but 'better' is not necessarily one of those.

Show respect for everyone regardless of their station in life. When you demonstrate respect it will be reflected back to you.

> "The world of employer and employee, like that of master and slave, debases both."
>
> Edward Abbey

Carrying through with the concept of offering your respect to all, Abbey refers to the unique personal relationship between a manager and an employee.

The manager who assumes the airs of arrogant self-importance debases both his employee and himself. The employee who cowers in slavish mode does the same.

Very few sayings in life are as valid as *'All things in moderation'*. And in this dance of a relationship between a boss and a worker, it holds true as well. Strive for a more even keeled understanding between you and your employees. Aim to work together toward a common goal but with the silent acknowledgement that YOU are the leader and decision maker. It is already obvious to the employee that you are. There is no need to remind them or bully them into submission with it.

A manager who is drunk with his own power will miss no opportunity to lord it over his workers. Doing so, damages egos and creates unnecessary friction. Employees' motivation to do well is lost in the enmity between the two parties. Instead of ordering people to do a task, simply point out that it needs to be done and suggest they be just the one to do it. Your position of authority is not questioned. Be gentle with your orders. A 'suggestion' is recognized for the order that it is but the show of respect will make the employee work all the harder.

"The magic formula that successful businesses have discovered is to treat customers like guests and employees like people."

Tom Peters

Peters is so tongue in cheek here that you probably read it twice to make sure you did not miss some gem of wisdom. It IS wise. And, in its own simple way, profound.

Somewhere in our mad rush to create higher profits, we have forgotten the basics and disregarded common courtesy. Peters is reminding us that business does not have to be confusing and complex. Simply treat people as you wish to be treated yourself.

Treat your customers like guests. Would you argue with a guest in your home? Would you try to sell a guest on purchasing something of questionable value? Would you tell a guest to wait while you do something you feel is more important? Perhaps you would but you would know immediately that it was bad form and improper. Yet, in business, we disagree with customers over issues; we sometimes offer low value for higher prices; and we put callers on hold while we attend to some other task.

Treat your employees like people. Do you 'move' them around the office like chess pieces? Do you herd them like cattle into meetings? Do you think of them as 'bodies' as you arbitrarily make schedules?

Keep it simple. Treat all people with respect and common courtesy, be they customers or employees. Your customers will be better motivated to buy and your employees will be incentivized to perform at their best.

"The best umpire is the one who isn't even noticed."
                          Many Baseball fans

Tis true in a business sense too. Excellent managers are able to motivate their people so well that all of the daily work goes on whether they are present or not. When you can reach the point where every employee is firing on all cylinders and staying productive even when you are not observing them, then you have arrived.

But, of course, it is more than just getting good productivity during your absence. It is instilling each employee with a strong sense of duty and responsibility. It is ingraining in each of them the feeling that doing their job at the highest level is the only way they want to work. It is reaching the point where everyone is on a mission and no force is going to stop them.

In many ways, you want to strive to field a team of self-motivated individuals who are busy all day because they want to be. You should be as unnoticed as the good ump who calls balls and strikes in anonymity and lets the game unfold as it will. Ideally, you should be able to stand in the middle of your office and simply watch all the activity around you. People hustling and rushing and trying their best because they are on a mission and you, Ms. Manager, are just a little bit irrelevant.

In the end, you do not want to be 'The Man'. You do not want to be the puller of strings or the daily decision maker. You want your team to be inspired to work hard for their own sake and empowered to make the decisions that are necessary.

When you are invisible, you are the most effective motivator and best manager of all.

> "Put me in coach! I can do it!"
> Thousands of youngsters

There is no greater show of respect than to give someone an opportunity. When you show that you trust an employee and are willing to grant them some authority and power to tackle a job, you are paying the highest compliment.

Just as many Little Leaguers have clamored for the chance to get an at bat or play centerfield, your employees hunger for the chance to show what they can do. They may be far more subtle and low-key than a Little Leaguer but the yearning is still there.

But trusting and bestowing power are scary steps to take in the business world. Often the downside seems far worse than the upside. So often, in fact, that many times it is not done at all. Many managers will just think to themselves that they are better off doing it all themselves. The prospect of failure by an underling is daunting and the potential losses often dissuade even the heartiest of us.

That failure to delegate and trust is common and it is OK. That is, it is OK if you never want to move further up the ladder. It is OK if you are willing to accept the status quo. It is OK if you would rather stagnate than grow.

But if you want growth, both for your business and for you as a business professional, respect your employees enough to give them a chance. Take it slowly. Dole out some smaller tasks with limited authority as you watch who can handle it and who is ready for more. Create some new roles and let someone spread their wings. When you provide opportunities, you are aggressively building a better team and paving your own path to the bigger and the better.

ALL WORK IS HONORABLE, STEVE …

It was spring in Cincinnati. Leaves were sprouting, baseball season was starting and hope sprung eternal. Except not for Steve. It seemed his head hung a little lower than usual and hope was in short supply.

Steve was 19, a part time cargo handler for Federal Express at the CVG airport in Northern Kentucky. I was the new Station Manager and I was fairly preoccupied with my own troubles. Bob, one of the dispatchers, approached me one day and said, *"You know, Steve is a good kid but he's pretty bummed out because he's too young to be a driver and he's tired of being a lowly cargo handler and part-time janitor. Maybe there is something we can do for him."*

Well, my ability to change Steve's situation was minimal. There simply were no other jobs he could be assigned to and no more hours to offer. After giving it some thought I sat down with Steve and talked with him about his situation. Steve felt embarrassed that he was part-time and doing 'lower-station work'. *"I hate being a janitor here. Sweeping the warehouse is so boring."*

I was at a loss for what to say to him so I fell back on something I had gleaned from a Kahlil Gibran book. I said, *"Steve, all work is honorable. I know that you'd like to do something else here but you are an excellent cargo loader and I know you don't believe it but the janitor duty is honorable work. You need to tackle it with enthusiasm and if you are going to clean up, then, damn it, be the best damn janitor in the world. I want you to make this place shine. When visitors come into town and view our operation, I want them to look at the warehouse and be stunned at its cleanliness. You're an artist. Make something beautiful."*

OK, I was thinking that I had never spewed such a crock before but, deep down, I believed it. I wanted him to feel a special pride in what he did and not to equate it with what he earned or what specific work he did. Everyone needs to feel that they are important so I added a few comments on how much I counted on him (and I **really did**, so that part was easy ...but we don't tell employees that often enough).

To my amazement, something clicked in Steve and he seemed to hold his head a bit higher after that. He continued his great work out on the tarmac and then stepped up his game in the warehouse. When I looked around, it truly did look stunning.

In December of that year, we had a Station party and awarded the 'Employee of the Year Award'. Steve won hands down and there was not a soul in the company who thought anyone deserved it more. I gave him his engraved trophy and he enjoyed the spotlight that night.

At the end of the year, FedEx moved me to Chicago and I said my goodbyes. A very short time later, I got a call from Bob, the dispatcher. He said that Steve had died in a car accident. I flew back to Cincy to attend the services. His father approached me and through teary eyes, said, *"That trophy was the pride of Steve's life. I can't tell you how much it meant to him and to us."*

As a business owner or manager we sometimes forget how much of a difference we can make. Don't.

GB

> Work is love made visible.
> And if you cannot work with love but only with distaste, it is better that you should leave your work and sit at the gate of the temple and take alms of those who work with joy.
> For if you bake bread with indifference, you bake a bitter bread that feeds but half man's hunger.
> And if you grudge the crushing of the grapes, your grudge distils a poison in the wine.
> And if you sing though as angels, and love not the singing, you muffle man's ears to the voices of the day and the voices of the night.
>
> Kahlil Gibran

"Most folks are as happy as they make up their minds to be."
Abraham Lincoln

As we talk about motivating employees, it is not uncommon to confuse that with 'making employees happy'. The two are not the same thing. Lincoln knew that happiness is a state of mind and often has little or nothing to do with an individual's current personal circumstances.

Keep in mind that you are not responsible for making people happy. As a manager however, you are, responsible for creating a business atmosphere that would allow people to be happy ... if they so choose. If you focus on creating the right setting, hiring the right people, incentivizing, rewarding and respecting your employees, you are doing your job. Being the happiness fairy is not your role.

So what do you do when a competent employee is treated well but is still unhappy? There are two things you can do: First, talk with him and see if there is anything within your power that might change his attitude. Learn a bit more about him. As Lincoln also once said, *"I don't like that man. I must get to know him better."* Often it is hard to like someone who is unhappy so see if you can change that. Second, if that fails and you are confident you have done all in your limited power, move on. Focus your efforts on those issues you can control and affect.

People will generally be as happy as they want to be. That goes for you too. But as their leader, do your best to exude some visible measure of good will and cheerfulness, for if you are a good leader, your people will emulate you. Set a good example and everyone will be happier.

THERE WILL BE NO RAISE ...

Rudy stopped by my office one evening and asked if he could talk to me. He told me that it had been six months since his last raise and he thought he deserved another one.

Now Rudy was not a bad worker, but he was not terrific either. On top of that, the economy was in one of those down cycles in the '80's and I had put a freeze on all pay increases to try to hold the line on costs. I told him that and he was understandably disappointed. Rudy countered, *"Well, the company is making a profit, right?"*

"Yes," I responded, *"but not a big enough one."* Well that didn't go over very big and I was at a bit of a loss as to what more to say to him when I decided to take a chance.

I said, *"Rudy, let me tell you the how and why of this issue."* And then I proceeded to talk to him about the big picture. I talked to him about economics in general and how it related to our company. I explained how the banker was looking for us to make a minimum 8% profit margin and if we did not, there would be no more loans or lines of credit. Then I painted the picture for him of what the company would look like if I had no ability to borrow money. Paychecks might bounce if I could not use my line of credit in key moments. Making more equipment purchases would be out of the question. Growth costs more so there would be less chance of that. If you are not growing, you're dying and we don't want to go there. Yada yada yada.

When we were done, Rudy shook my hand and said, *"I get it now. No one ever explained that to me before. Thanks for leveling with me."*

It was still a NO; A long drawn-out NO. But by talking UP to my employee instead of down, his pain of rejection was eased and I learned a valuable lesson: Talk **up** to your employees. Tell the truth and tell it like it is.

GB

"Make no little plans; they have no magic to stir men's blood."
Daniel Burnham

Daniel Burnham was the primary architect of the 1893 Chicago World's Fair and key contributor of the "City Beautiful Movement". Burnham's comment is the final thought to this treatise on motivation.

It is easy to feel insignificant in this ever-changing world of ours; to feel small in the vast universe that is business today. People everywhere want to feel important, cared about, included and challenged. They yearn for greater meaning in their lives and their work. Leaders recognize that need and seek to help fill it.

If your organization does not have a Mission Statement that captures a shared dream, then create one. In some cases, large high profile companies actually set their goal as 'Changing the World'. That would be a big plan with the magic to stir men's blood. But most of us are not managing those companies. Many of us manage small companies with realistic but relatively modest goals. What can we do to create a little magic of our own?

Part of your job is to find that magic. To define what goals you can set that get your people excited: Expansion of more stores? Setting a performance record? Beating a superior competitor? Whatever it might be, discover it, reveal it, share it and enjoy the journey with your employees. Revel in the ups and downs. Face adversity with a stalwart spirit. Celebrate the minor triumphs as well as the great ones. But do it together.

SUMMARY:

As Peters said, it really is simple. Treat people with respect and you will be the leader you need to be.
- Look into your own soul. If you feel a lack of respect for your people, purge it and start again. If you feel it, you cannot hide it. Restructure your thinking.
- Do not assume a blatant upper hand with your employees. They already know you are the boss. There is no need to provide direction with a heavy hand.
- Treat both your customers and your workers with the kind of respect you would demand.
- Find a way to give your people some opportunities. Create roles, delegate duties, observe the results. Remember that you and the business will not grow when you are the only one wielding power and authority.
- You are the pace setter. If you are unhappy in your job, your employees will be too. Share some visible good cheer and help others down the same path.
- Give your people a larger goal to work for. Focus on the big picture and involve them in the grander plan. Both life and work are more exciting and rewarding when the magic stirs men's blood.

CHAPTER NINE

CONCLUSION

How far we have come! Since ancient peoples utilized slave labor to build great monuments to today when modern managers strive for success by building cohesive teamwork. In many ways, we have traded the yokes of authoritarian leadership for the science of motivation and we are the better for it.

You are a manager of people because you have shown some ability to communicate, cajole and sometimes coerce your employees to perform well. But you are a work in progress. As competent as you might be today, you know you can be more proficient tomorrow. Every day is a learning experience and you have both the desire and the skills to constantly improve.

Motivating people to do their jobs with greater and greater skill is a challenging role. And yes, people ultimately have to motivate themselves. Still, you are in a position to have super human influence on your employees and can affect their efforts with your daily actions. As you know, it is not a feat accomplished overnight. It is a long slow dance that starts with an application and proceeds with graceful subtlety. It is a well reinforced theme that surrounds you and your workers with a daily embrace. It is a mutual journey filled with both shared failure and success. And, in case you forgot, it all begins with you. YOU. No one else.

You have the will and knowledge to create the right atmosphere welcoming individual initiative and resourcefulness. You are the architect that builds the business with the foundation of the right employees. You are the leader who designs the greeting and training process to start your people out on the right foot. You are the one with the power to incentivize and reward properly. You are the deliverer of quality reviews and timely raises. You are the manager who brings your employees together by acting as the servant to them all. And you are the leader who respects all people for their unique and intrinsic value.

You are all those things or you can be soon. Be the leader you know in your heart that you can be. Build an organization that respects, recognizes, reinforces and rewards proper action. All this is within your power if only you will accept the responsibility.

And what happens when you do all this? What happens is a miracle of your own making. It is a company with a life of its own. It is a set of individuals who coalesce into a hard charging team. It is a company with momentum that drives to the goal line time and time again. And it is a unit of inspired, motivated, spirited and joyful employees who perform at their best; not because they've been ordered to but because they want to.

And YOU have the ability to bring this about. In the end, your duty is clear. Move the organization forward. That is best achieved by aligning your individual employees' enlightened self-interest with the company's goals and sharing the joys of the journey together. Make it a memorable voyage that lasts for years. Motivating your people properly is a long flight but it will take you to heights you cannot imagine.

A leader is best when people barely know he exists,
when his work is done, his aim fulfilled,
they will say: we did it ourselves!
Lao-Tzu

Gary Brose is available to make appearances at your next Corporate Event as a Keynote speaker, presenter or workshop leader. For current rates and more information, visit www.SmallBizSherpa.com

Also available by Gary Brose:

"BONUS YOUR WAY TO PROFITS!"
A Manager's Guide to Radical Pay Restructuring.

What is included in this book:

- The Eight Essential Elements of a Quality Bonus Program
- A detailed description of each element
- Examples of bonus programs that succeeded
- Examples of bonus programs that failed and why
- Step by Step instructions on how to design a quality bonus program
- Sample memos to your staff
- Samples of ways to handle objections from the staff
- A detailed explanation of how to transition from a traditional pay model to a bonus-based program

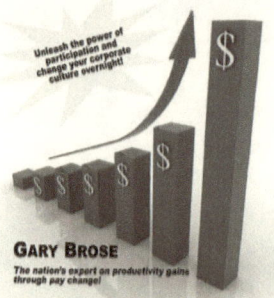

Written by Gary Brose in a no-nonsense business fashion. Gary believes in getting right to the point and he has written a book that any business owner or manager can finish in one sitting.

Immediately upon finishing this book, you will be able to begin designing your own bonus-based compensation structure that breathes new life into your company and has the power to add significantly to your bottom line!

If you could improve profits by $5,000 a year, would you pay $500 for that? I'm betting you would! "Bonus Your Way to Profits" will show you how to cut payroll costs or increase sales and productivity to do just that and more!

Imagine cutting payroll cost by just 2%. On a payroll of $22,000 per month, you would save well over $5,000 yearly. "Bonus Your Way to Profits" does NOT cost $500! It retails at $19.95 **and it's a smart deal at TEN times the price.**

Available now at www.SmallBizSherpa.com

www.ingramcontent.com/pod-product-compliance
Lightning Source LLC
Chambersburg PA
CBHW021956170526
45157CB00003B/1008